Beyond Early Literacy

For early childhood classrooms—where curriculum is increasingly shaped by standards and teachers are pressed for time—*Beyond Early Literacy* offers a literacy method that goes beyond simply developing language arts skills. Known as Shared Journal, this process promotes young children's learning across content areas—including their communication and language abilities, writing skills, sense of community, grasp of diverse social and cultural worlds, and understanding of history, counting, numeracy, and time. Pairing interactive talk with individual writing in the classroom community, this rich method develops the whole child.

Special features include:

- Sample lesson plans, rubrics, and templates throughout the book
- Children's artifacts, including examples of oral and written work
- Teacher accounts examining the use of Shared Journal in the classroom, including strategies and suggestions
- A companion website with templates, additional resources, video clips of in-classroom teaching, and examples of exciting ways to use new technologies

This two-part book is first framed by current theory and research about children's cognitive, language, and literacy development, and an extensive body of research and case studies on the efficacy of the method. The second part features strategies from on-the-ground teachers who have used the process with their students, and explores how Shared Journal can be used with new technologies, can meet standards, and can be appropriate for diverse populations of children. This is a fantastic resource for use in early childhood education courses in emergent literacy, language arts, and curriculum.

Janet B. Taylor is Wayne T. Smith Distinguished Professor Emeritus of Early Childhood Education at Auburn University.

Nancy Amanda Branscombe is Assistant Professor of Early Childhood Education at Athens State University.

Jan Gunnels Burcham is Professor of Early Childhood Education and Fletcher Distinguished Chair of Teacher Education at Columbus State University.

Lilli Land is a recipient of the NAESP National Distinguished Principal Award for Alabama and is currently an education consultant.

Beyond Early Literacy

A Balanced Approach to Developing the Whole Child

JANET B. TAYLOR, NANCY AMANDA BRANSCOMBE,
JAN GUNNELS BURCHAM, AND LILLI LAND

with

SANDY ARMSTRONG, ANGELA CARR,
AND ALLYSON MARTIN

Routledge
Taylor & Francis Group

NEW YORK AND LONDON

First published 2011
by Routledge
270 Madison Avenue, New York, NY 10016

Simultaneously published in the UK
by Routledge
2 Park Square, Milton Park, Abingdon, Oxon OX14 4RN

Routledge is an imprint of the Taylor & Francis Group, an informa business

© 2011 Taylor & Francis

Typeset in Sabon and Neue Helvetica by Book Now Ltd, London
Printed and bound in the United States of America on acid-free paper by Edwards Brothers, Inc.

Library of Congress Cataloging in Publication Data
Beyond early literacy: a balanced approach to developing the whole child / by Janet B. Taylor ... [et al.].
    p. cm.
Includes bibliographical references.
1. Child development—Handbooks, manuals, etc. 2. Child rearing—Handbooks, manuals, etc. 3. Education, Preschool—Curricula—Handbooks, manuals, etc. 4. Education, Preschool—Activity programs—Handbooks, manuals, etc. 5. Classroom learning centers—Handbooks, manuals, etc. I. Taylor, Janet B.

HQ767.9.B48 2010
372.01′9—dc22   2010017578

ISBN13: 978–0–415–87443–4 (hbk)
ISBN13: 978–0–415–87444–1 (pbk)
ISBN13: 978–0–203–85311–5 (ebk)

Dedication

This book is dedicated to all my wonderful students who have used and helped me research Shared Journal.

Janet B. Taylor

I dedicate my work with this book to my dear friends, who happen to be cousins, Nancy Claire Edwards, Eugenia Branscomb Hobday, Penelope Branscomb Leggett, and Kenneth Lauren McMillan. I also dedicate it to my dear friend Lavaris Demar Thomas.

Nancy Amanda Branscombe

I dedicate this book to my family: my parents, Dr. Wheeler and Betty Gunnels, who have encouraged and supported me through every step of my life; my sister, Julie Gunnels Nordeman, her husband, Doug, and their daughters, Katie and Emma—they are my sunshine; and most of all, to my husband, Andy, who believes in me and makes life a wonderful journey. I love you all.

Jan Gunnels Burcham

I would like to thank Dr. Janet Taylor for all of the support she has given me as an educator and for her help as we began the first year of Shared Journal. What an exciting adventure it has been! My appreciation goes to Darcy Caldwell for collaborating with me in our research and to Allyson Martin for being fun, flexible, and encouraging as we worked together in our endeavors for children. Also, I would like to thank the parents, teachers, school staff, and administrators I have worked with over the years. You have been an important part of Shared Journal. In addition, I want to thank my mother, family, friends, and best friend, Kimberly, for their love and support. Most importantly, I dedicate this book to the children I have worked with during my career. They have been the stars in Shared Journal and the passion in my life.

Lilli Land

Contents

Illustrations

Figures

Tables

Preface

Overview of the Book

The goal of this book is to provide teacher educators, classroom teachers, professional development personnel, and graduate and undergraduate students with a theoretically grounded research process called Shared Journal that enables children to learn all subject matter in the same natural way they learn to walk and talk during the early years of their lives. Additionally, this book will introduce a variety of ways teachers can implement and use the Shared Journal process to foster children's development throughout all of the content areas. Shared Journal uses interactive talk within the context of the classroom as an incentive and a vehicle for helping children come to understand and record events from their life experiences by drawing and reconstructing them into modes of discourse. Through participation in the process, children learn to reflect not only on their own experiences but also on those of their classmates, thereby developing their abilities to consider others' perspectives.

The book is divided into two parts. The first provides a theoretical framework or foundation about children's understandings of their own writing process, their use of Shared Journal as a means of understanding and developing their own writing abilities, and their understandings of their social and cultural worlds. This information is offered through research studies done by the four main authors and their students.

The second part details the implementation of Shared Journal in multiple settings. This implementation is presented through the stories of researchers and reflective practitioners who have used Shared Journal with their students for over 10 years. Although some of the teachers have not formally researched their use of Shared Journal, they have used reflection and questioning to study children's learning in and reactions to the process.

Notes from the Authors

The authors of *Beyond Early Literacy: A Balanced Approach to Developing the Whole Child* bring different perspectives about Shared Journal.

Dr. Janet B. Taylor

Shared Journal was born out of my discontent with how initial reading and writing were, and continue to be, taught. As an Early Childhood Teacher Educator, I had studied Piagetian theory through coursework before and after earning my Ph.D. and traveled to Geneva, Switzerland to study with Hermina Sinclair at the Geneva Institute. Therefore, I was interested in developing a practice based on theoretical explanations of how young children learn rather than on how the subject matter should be taught. This required the identification and selection of constructivist tenets that seemed most applicable to learning, and examining how those tenets could be applied to a practice that would not only allow for the child's construction of a system of written language and an authentic literary voice, but would also allow for the construction of knowledge in all content areas.

Language learning is part of the development of the semiotic function, and the child's ability to use conventional letters to represent what he knows grows out of a continued differentiation and coordination between the ideas to be expressed and the means by which to express them. This raised many questions in my mind. How do children come to know that what they have to say is relevant to others? How do they learn to appraise the stories they have to tell and the way in which they tell them? What earlier schemes do children have available for literary discourse? These questions helped me begin to explore how we could teach literacy in a way that would help children become makers and users of literature.

Two intriguing ideas emerged from the theory. The first was the idea that when knowledge of the signified (the event, object, or story) is shared among individuals, they can use that knowledge to collaboratively construct a relationship between it and its signifier (pictures and words). Thus, if what was to be drawn or written was shared and known in some form by each child, they could collaborate on how to draw, write, or read about the event. The second theoretical idea was that social interaction facilitates cognitive development (Perret-Clermont, 1980), that socio-cognitive conflict is a factor in that development (Kamii, 1985), and that this kind of group interaction is most effective at the stage when schemes are first being developed and refined (Doise & Mugny, 1984).

Using these ideas, I added a component to the practice that differentiated it from individual journal writing. This component provided the time and place for children to discuss, debate, and determine the topic they thought most appropriate for their daily entry. Through this kind of sharing and negotiation, children could come to know which of the stories in their lives connected them to the others in their world, and, at the same time, differentiated them from those same others. Additionally, I thought that their retelling of events out of past experiences and listening to others tell their stories would help them come to know themselves and their world more fully.

These ideas have been shown to be true through a significant body of research and the testimonies of countless teachers, who have implemented the practice at the preschool level, in every elementary grade level, in junior and senior high schools, and in university classes. In this book we discuss all of the different ways Shared Journal can be used in classrooms to help children grow and learn in all of the curriculum areas. Although this text is designed primarily for those interested in early childhood education, the Shared Journal process has been successfully used in Junior and Senior High classes and with undergraduate students in Colleges of Education.

Dr. Nancy Amanda Branscombe

I began my teaching career as a secondary English teacher. After several years of teaching high school composition, I decided to attend Middlebury College's summer Language School and study the teaching of writing at Bread Loaf School of English. Over the next four summers, I had the opportunity to have Dixie Goswami, James Britton, Nancy Martin, Courtney Cazden, and Shirley Brice Heath as some of my teachers. During that time, they encouraged me to become a teacher researcher. Heath even collaborated with me in a year-long ethnographic study of at-risk ninth graders' knowledge of the language in their environments. Several of the ninth graders either had children or were the primary caregivers for their younger siblings. Because of this, Heath and I did an early literacy project that involved having one student, Charlene Thomas, read bedtime stories to her two infant sons. This project piqued my interest in how young children learn language and literacy. As a result of this research and a change in directions in my career, I decided to earn my doctorate in early literacy.

Because I lived in Auburn, Alabama at the time, I decided to attend Auburn University for my doctoral studies. There I met Dr. Janet Taylor, who would later become my mentor and major professor for my doctoral studies. She introduced me to Shared Journal by inviting me to assist her in gathering data for her second year of research in Alexander City, Alabama. My task was to administer a spelling test, interview children, and observe teachers as they used Shared Journal. Joanne Terrell, Brenda Sharman, Barbara Thompson, and Misty Sanders, who were kindergarten teachers and participants in the research project, took the time to teach me all aspects of Shared Journal. In addition to their teaching, their kindergarten children offered even more help. After more than four months of training with the teachers and their kindergarten children, as well as the analysis of the research data, I knew that I wanted to use Shared Journal in my own classroom.

Because Dr. Taylor believed in the importance of early childhood teacher educators having experience in the classroom, I taught kindergarten in a small, rural community close to Auburn. Needless to say, one of my most valued classroom strategies was Shared Journal. After completing my degree, I directed several preschool and child development centers at other universities. At each university, I introduced Shared Journal to my preschool teachers and asked them to use it with their three-, four- and young five-year-olds. They were equally delighted and successful with Shared Journal. In addition to my work with Shared Journal at the preschool level, I've continued to research it in kindergarten and elementary classrooms.

Dr. Jan Gunnels Burcham

My experience with Shared Journal began when I was an undergraduate in the Early Childhood Teacher Education program at Auburn University. I had the good fortune to be in Dr. Janet Taylor's classes, where she helped us understand the theoretical support for and process of Shared Journal. In 1985, when I began my first full-time teaching position in a kindergarten classroom, I knew that I wanted to include Shared Journal in my teaching. Little did I know at that time how important it would become throughout my career. I have now implemented or worked with teachers implementing Shared Journal from the kindergarten level all the way through higher education classrooms as well as in summer enrichment programs and in special pull-out intervention programs. I have also conducted research as well as directed Master's and Education Specialist students' research about Shared Journal.

As a classroom teacher, I implemented Shared Journal in varied ways. I started by implementing it when I could work it into my overcrowded day. Because I realized its benefits, I increased it to at least two times per week. Finally, I committed to doing Shared Journal daily in my classroom. There was no comparison in the rate and amount of development and learning I saw once I committed to implementing Shared Journal daily. It also became extremely important to my students. If there was ever a day when they thought we might not get to our journal entries, they always came to me to saying, "We have to get our journals done. We have stories to tell!"

Shared Journal was an important part of my dissertation research (which is included in Chapter Ten – Shared Journal with Special Groups). I have also worked with several Master's and Education Specialist students as they implemented Shared Journal in their classrooms and conducted research. Without fail, they have found that Shared Journal is a powerful addition to their curriculums. Its impact goes far beyond the development of literacy, though it is ideal for literacy acquisition. Perhaps most significantly, it provides a wonderful way to develop community in the classroom and promote students' socio-emotional development. As I work in higher education now, teaching pre-service and in-service educators, I always explain the following: if I could only select one approach to use in my teaching (at any level), it would be Shared Journal. It is that powerful and meaningful to me, as a teacher, and to my students.

Dr. Lilli Land

With a new emphasis on literacy development in my kindergarten classroom curriculum, I sought new methods to introduce literacy in developmentally appropriate ways. In August of 1984, I attended an Early Childhood Conference in Montgomery, Alabama to find innovative ways to improve my teaching. After the general assembly, I noticed a session on writing for grades K–2. I was not sure how I would apply writing to my kindergarten students, but when I saw that Dr. Janet Taylor was conducting the session, I knew that she would show me how this would apply in my kindergarten curriculum. At that moment, I made the decision to enter this session, and this choice proved to be one of the best and most important decisions I ever made in my career as an educator.

In this small group session, the more I listened the more interested I became. This activity seemed very similar to other language experience approaches because children talked about events in their lives and then wrote about these experiences. If language experience approaches were good strategies for teaching reading, then what a great addition to the curriculum Shared Journal would be. It would serve as an additional instructional strategy for developing language skills that would help my children learn to read. Also, I realized that Shared Journal would not only help my children learn to read and write but would also help them construct notions of time, because the journal had one page for each school day of the month.

As a classroom teacher, I felt that I could do this. Shared Journal was an instructional strategy that did not require a great deal of planning and would be easy to implement. Just thinking about the children writing every day about real life experiences excited me. I was sold. Shared Journal would be the new strategy I would use with my children when school began. At the time, I was not aware that this decision would change my teaching and my students' learning for the rest of my career.

The Collaboration

Because of the very nature of Shared Journal, a book about this method had to be a collaborative venture. Janet Taylor is the senior author of the book. She conceptualized, designed and taught about Shared Journal. As a result of her work, the other authors have implemented, researched, written about, and taught the process. Thus, the listing of these authors is an alphabetical and nonhierarchical listing of authors. Three classroom teachers, Sandy Armstrong, Angela Carr, and Allyson Martin, were invited to be a part of this writing venture because of their specific work with Shared Journal. Jan Gunnels Burcham filled the role of liaison with the publisher in addition to her writing responsibilities.

Acknowledgements

We would like to acknowledge the support of our editor, Heather Jarrow, and our clerical assistant and proofreader, Altamese Stroud-Hill. They were both very supportive and helpful throughout the process of writing this book. There have been many people who contributed to the development of Shared Journal. These include students from undergraduate and graduate courses as well as teachers in schools with whom we collaborated and supervised student teachers. While it is impossible to mention all those individuals by name, we would like to specifically acknowledge the assistance of the following outstanding teachers: Debbie Blackmon, Mary Boos, Darcy Caldwell, Denise Dark, Rosalind Fuller, Leisha Hayes, Sandy Little, Misty Sanders, Brenda Sharman, JoAnn Terrell, Barbara Thompson, and Ronda Peacock Ware. They provided continuous support and encouragement, they asked questions and made Shared Journal even better, and they provided many of the rich examples that made this book possible. It is our hope that, along with us, they and the readers of this book will continue to share our stories and our lives through Shared Journal.

part one
The Child as Learner

Part One examines all aspects of children's learning, particularly through Shared Journal. It presents the theoretical underpinnings of how children construct relationships, understand their cultures, and make sense of the physical world through their daily interactions with others in their immediate environments. This theoretical understanding is instrumental in the effectiveness of Shared Journal.

Chapter 1, "The Child as Learner," utilizes a constructivist framework to summarize the child's early cognitive and language learning. It includes sections on difficulties with language learning, English language learners, and the adult's role in early learning.

Chapter 2, "The Process of Shared Journal," details the procedures used to prepare for and implement Shared Journal. It explains each step and offers examples and suggestions for implementation.

Chapter 3, "Learning in the Communicative Arts," and Chapter 6, "Learning in the Content Areas," examine Shared Journal within the context of the school curriculum. Chapter 3 is devoted to explaining how Shared Journal addresses the Communicative Arts, which include the language arts of speaking, listening, reading, and writing and the visual arts of viewing, designing, creating, and producing. It also documents all of the communicative abilities children develop through participating in Shared Journal on a daily basis. Chapter 6 identifies and documents the content, strategies, and processes children learn in the social studies, mathematics, science, and technology as they participate in Shared Journal. It recounts how children come to better understand themselves, their classmates, and their communities by engaging in the daily use of Shared Journal. In addition, it explains how children and teachers can use Shared Journal stories to embark on studies in science, mathematics, and the social studies.

Chapter 4, "The Reading/Writing Connection," explicates how the intimately connected processes of reading and writing are learned through the daily process of Shared Journal. It documents how participation in Shared Journal fosters growth in the development of phonemic awareness, phonics, oral language/vocabulary, fluency, and comprehension. Furthermore, it explains how Shared Journal fosters the natural interaction and integration of reading and writing for authentic purposes.

Chapter 5, "Developing the Narrative Voice," defines narrative voice as well as describes the role of the narrative voice in helping the child create credible stories that others value and enjoy. It also documents how children experiment with and use literacy constructions and devices to create their stories. Finally, it offers evidence of how personal narratives provide the foundation for children's advancement from oracy to literacy.

one
The Child as Learner

The purpose of this introductory chapter is to document what and how young children learn during the first few years of their lives. It is designed to help teachers think about this early learning and about the scientific explanations of how and why this learning takes place. This introductory chapter provides the theoretical and scientific framework for understanding the success of the content found in this book. This framework is based on the work of Jean Piaget (1983).

Young children learn to think though their own actions on objects and their interactions with others. This kind of learning is natural and comfortable for children. They develop theories about the world in which they live as they act on objects and discover what happens through those interactions. This motivates them to continue to experiment with the objects. These interactions foster children's continuing abilities to think about and reflect on the world in which they live without any kind of formal instruction.

The ability to reason develops through four major stages that include the sensorimotor, preoperational, concrete operational and formal operational (see Table 1.1). This development proceeds through these stages in order, but the rate of development varies according to the individual. This chapter will focus on the earlier stages, since they are the foundation of thought.

Within each stage, children construct mental relationships that form the structure of their thought (Piaget, 1969). Recent brain research provides confirming information about the biological structures that Piaget identified earlier (Rushton, 2001). Scans show that the brain is made up of neurons connected at the synapses to form "neural pathways." These neural pathways are consistent with what Piaget described as the construction of mental relationships that form the foundation of learning. Wesson (2003) explains that, when new learning occurs, a corresponding neurophysiologic connection is created in the brain.

Children learn to use language to communicate what they have come to know about their worlds. For example, they learn most of their native language without anyone specifically teaching it to them. From the moment they utter their first cries, children begin learning language by using the sounds they can make to imitate the voices around them. The specific language they begin to learn and the rate at which they learn it depend on the home and community language into which they are born. Scientific theories about how children learn language differ. Some linguists (Chomsky, 1975; Pinker, 1994) hold that children have innate, language-specific abilities that facilitate and

TABLE 1.1 Piaget's Stages of Cognitive Development

Stage	Description
Sensorimotor (Infancy)	During this stage (which has six sub-stages), the learner constructs knowledge about himself and his environment through motor and reflex actions. Intelligence is demonstrated through motor activity without the use of symbols. Knowledge of the world is limited (but developing) because it is based on physical interactions and experiences. Learners acquire object permanence. Physical development (mobility) allows the learner to begin developing new intellectual abilities. Some symbolic (language) abilities are developed at the end of this stage.
Preoperational (Toddler and Early Childhood)	In this stage (which has two sub-stages), intelligence is demonstrated through the use of symbols, language use matures, and memory and imagination are developed, but thinking is done in a nonlogical, nonreversible manner. Egocentric thinking predominates.
Concrete Operational (Elementary and Early Adolescence)	In this stage, intelligence is demonstrated through logical and systematic manipulation of symbols related to concrete objects. Operational thinking develops (mental actions that are reversible). Egocentric thought diminishes.
Formal Operational (Adolescence and Adulthood)	In this stage, intelligence is demonstrated through the logical use of symbols related to abstract concepts. The learner is capable of hypothetical and deductive reasoning. Many people do not think formally during adulthood.

constrain language learning, while others (MacWhinney, 1999; Piaget & Inhelder, 1969) hold that language learning results from general cognitive abilities and the social interaction between young language learners and their surrounding communities. While the topic of whether language learning is innate or the result of general cognitive abilities remains debatable, the processes by which children acquire language are well-researched and have been expanded to include research on early brain development. Interestingly, this recent research into the developing brain also supports the Piagetian theory about language development. For example, researchers have documented that the developing brain needs interaction with other people and objects (Perry & Pollard, 1997). Piaget identified this as social interaction, a process that is strongly supported in this text.

Language learning includes four different kinds of development. These are phonological development (the ability to hear, discriminate, and produce the phonemes or sounds of the language), semantic development (the ability to use words to make meaning), syntactic development (the ability to use word-combining rules), and pragmatic development (the ability to understand the conventional ways language is used). Most of this development takes place during the first five years of a child's life.

Early Cognition and Language Learning

Birth to Six Months

Early language learning refers to the learning that occurs during the first two years of life. The cognitive correlate of the early language-learning period is the sensorimotor period of intellectual development (Piaget, 1970). During this period, infants think, not in the way we know the term, but rather by using all of their senses and some motoric activity to come to know about the world into which they were born. During this time the infants learn to lift their heads, turn over, and sit up with support. They begin to differentiate objects to be sucked or grasped. For example, they may reject the pacifier if they want milk.

Infants begin to learn language as they listen and start to make and manipulate the sounds in their environment. They experiment with all of the speech sounds that are possible for humans to make. Early in their development, they are able to discriminate between speech and environmental sounds, and they play with the different rhythmic and intonation patterns of the human voice. They learn to use different cries depending on what they want, and adults quickly respond to those they recognize.

As infants listen to adults in their immediate environments, they begin to imitate the speech sounds they hear. By six to seven weeks of age, they are able to produce long drawn out vowel sounds through their cooing. They respond to a distinctive kind of talk that many adults adopt when they talk to infants. This talk, sometimes referred to as motherese, uses a soft loving tone and a slower more exaggerated form of speech. As infants listen to this talk, they begin to engage in turn-taking with the adult speaker by cooing and gurgling. They are able to communicate their feelings through laughing, fussing, and crying, and they respond to being talked to by making noises and moving both arms and legs.

Six to Eight Months

Cognitively, infants at this age build on earlier learning and begin to act intentionally and are active in their home or other environments. For example, as they lie in their beds, they use developing eye–hand coordination to swing their arms and make the mobile move. They also learn to repeat actions to produce certain effects. For example, if they are on the floor, they may push the ball over and over to see where it goes.

After six or seven months of experimentation with speech sounds, infant vocalizations change so that they begin to use mainly the speech sounds of the language into which they are being raised, and they begin babbling using consonant–vowel syllables. Additionally, they begin to lose the ability to produce those sounds that are not part of their native language (Lindfors, 1991). This is particularly important for teachers to understand as they begin to work with children who use a dialect that differs from Standard English or for whom English is a second language, as these children may be unable to produce and/or discriminate many of the English speech sounds. However, when young children are exposed to more than one language in the home from birth, they are not confused, nor do they experience language delays. The outcome of experiencing multiple languages from birth is that children differentiate between the two languages and experience normal vocabulary growth in both languages (Petitto, Katerelos, Levy, Gauna, Tetreault, & Ferraro, 2001).

Eight to Twelve Months

Infants at this age are still in the sensorimotor stage of development. During this time, children continually seek new ways and actions to explore their environments. They have learned to sit up without assistance, crawl across the floor, and to stand without help. Most learn to walk with adult support and are able to use their thumbs and fore-fingers to grasp and hold objects. This ability provides many opportunities for them to explore a variety of objects of different shapes and sizes.

Also, during this time, infants begin to control their sound patterns so that their syllables become more adult in nature. Their babbling becomes more varied by using strings of sounds that begin with a consonant followed by a vowel, such as "mama" or "gaga," and their speech utterances begin to conform to the intonation features of the language they are learning through their use of stress, rhythm, and pitch. Parents often respond to this kind of babbling and act as if they are having a conversation with the infant, and they repeat what the child says to encourage the child to say it again. These parental interactions are essential, as they help the infant move from isolated sounds to the use of sound patterns that symbolize a specific meaning (Anning & Edwards, 1999). By ten months, infants begin to respond more eagerly to words that name the objects that are of interest to them (Pruden, Golinkoff, & Hennon, 2006). Thus, at this early age, infants are learning many new words even though they do not yet speak them. This leads to the beginning of the infants' use of one-word expressions that may have different meanings depending on the context. For example, "Go" may mean, "I want to go with you," or it may mean, "Please, Mommy, don't go." The meaning of the word is conveyed through the infant's actions and intonations.

Twelve to Eighteen Months

Cognitively, these infants are in the latter part of the sensorimotor stage. They have learned to walk by themselves, are able to climb stairs and on to furniture, to roll balls, and to use eating utensils such as spoons and cups. This improved mobility allows them more opportunities to coordinate their reflexes in relation to objects. Additionally, they are able to feed themselves using their fingers. These infants enjoy interactions with their caregivers while eating, diaper changing, and playing.

From twelve to eighteen months of age, infants begin to develop understandings of objects, places, actions, and people and produce words that are holophrastic in nature, in that one word represents a whole idea. They use these holophrastic words to name people or objects, to express actions, such as "go" or "eat," and to express negation, such as "no" or "not." During this period their vocabulary grows from the use of a few words to the use of around 30 words, most of which are nouns but also include some verbs and adjectives. Their set of speech sounds begins to include the use of diphthongs such as the "oy" in boy and the "ow" in cow. They develop the ability to engage in verbal turn-taking and are able to understand and follow simple directions like "come back" or "stop now." By the end of this period, they are no longer able to distinguish sounds that are not of the language or languages they are acquiring.

Eighteen Months to Two Years

In this period, toddlers' ability to move differentiates them from infants. During this time, there is rapid growth and development in their abilities to walk and run so that they are able to participate in a number of different kinds of activities like playing, jumping, and running games. Their thinking is moving from the sensorimotor state to preoperational thought that includes the beginnings of the ability to reverse thought. This includes their ability to bring to mind images of past events and things that are not present and their desire to play with other children. They are becoming aware of rules and are not concerned with winning, just playing with others.

From eighteen months to two years, toddlers acquire more simple verbs such as "play" or "eat" and are able to produce many consonantal sounds, most vowel sounds, and are able to use intonation to ask questions. Additionally, they can respond to hearing the names of different body parts and point to them when asked. During this period, children will develop a speaking vocabulary of about 150 words and a listening vocabulary of approximately 400 to 500 words. They become able to ask questions by using a rising intonation and are beginning to understand and use grammatical morphemes added to words to denote plurals (my friends), possessives (mama's dress), and tenses (I'm going).

As they continue to experiment with speech, not only through imitation, but also through their own ability to devise and use forms that are not used by adults (Genishi, 1988), they begin to combine words like "no milk" and "go bye." These word combinations become more common and more complex and, by the end of this period, they will have developed a mean length utterance (Brown, 1973) of two words. This mean length utterance is determined by finding the child's average number of words per utterance. According to Brown, the increasing average length of utterances is a sign of increasing complexity in the child's use of words.

By about two years of age, toddlers begin to experiment with a variety of different ways their words can function (Halliday, 1978). They use the instrumental function to ensure their needs are met, i.e. "more milk," and they use the regulatory function to control others, i.e. "no go." They use the personal-interactional function when they talk about themselves and their feelings, i.e. "see me." When they question (i.e. "me go?"), they are using the heuristic function, and when they play (i.e. "silly me"), they are using the imaginative function. When they tell others their names, they are using the informative function. However, they are just beginning to experiment with these different functions and will grow to use them in a more sophisticated manner as their language continues to develop.

Representation and the Semiotic Function

Children's representational development provides the transition from the sensorimotor stage into the preoperational stage of thought. Important structural changes in the brain allow for this new representational thought to occur. Language is the ability to use signs to represent ideas and actions. It is the most advanced form of the semiotic function that develops from earlier forms of representation that include play, imitation, symbols, and mental images. Piaget's identification of the semiotic function that children use to make and provide meaning for themselves and others is the foundation on which the Shared Journal process has been designed. The semiotic or representational function involves the ability to mentally represent an object, event, or idea through the use of an image, symbol, or sign and begins when the child is around two years of age (Piaget, 1962). Representation refers to the ability to bring to mind things that are no longer present or actions that occurred some time in the past, which is acquired as the child engages in play and imitation. This ability is initiated when the child begins the use of deferred imitation and develops, through mental images, to the use of symbols and signs to signify actions or objects.

Deferred Imitation

The earliest form of representational ability is deferred imitation or imitation that occurs in the absence of the thing being represented. Young toddlers, less than two years old, make use of deferred imitation when they use a convenient object like a block to represent a train as they push it along the rug saying "choo-choo." Deferred imitation also occurs as children imitate the behavior of an action they have previously observed. For example, a child may go to the porch where he had previously seen a cat stalking a squirrel and move his arms and legs as if to imitate the cat stalking its prey or may take a set of keys to the door to imitate the actions of unlocking the door. This kind of deferred imitation is significant in that it documents the child's ability to bring to mind or think about past actions and objects that are no longer present.

Symbolic or Pretend Play

Pretend play is an important development in the semiotic function that begins to occur around the age of three. In this more advanced kind of symbolic use, children work together, take on the roles of others, and agree on the use of objects to represent their ideas. For example, it is common to see a child in the preschool classroom pick up a block and use it as a telephone to "call" another child, who picks up another block to answer the "call." This more advanced form of representation requires agreement among players on what the objects and actions symbolize in order to carry out the play. This kind of collaborative play suggests that the children have constructed shared meanings that bring about these coordinated actions (Stambak & Sinclair, 1993).

Drawing

Drawing is midway between pretend play and the mental image in that, like play, it serves as an enjoyable activity and, like the mental image, it is a representation of something held in mind. The child's early drawings start with scribbles. Once the scribbles seem to resemble something known, the child discovers this resemblance and names the picture. If the child tries to remake the same picture from memory at a later time, drawing becomes imitation and image representation.

Although children typically draw what they know rather than what they see (Piaget & Inhelder, 1969), these drawings are primarily realistic in their intent. Children's early drawings lack perspective in that their facial profiles will include both eyes, and their chimneys will be perpendicular to the roof instead of the ground. Up until the age of four, children's spatial understandings are topological in nature. Because of this, all of their geometric shapes are drawn as closed circles and crosses and arcs are made with an open curve (Gruber & Voneche, 1995). Through continued drawing, children begin to make their scribbles more realistic, in that they have characteristics that are representational; for example, a house may have two sides and a roof (see Figure 1.1).

FIGURE 1.1　Sample of Representational Drawing

Drawing helps children construct concrete ways to represent what they know. This is very powerful in the development of the use of symbols and is directly related to the process of learning to use more abstract symbols to read and write.

Mental Images

Mental images are internalized forms of representation. They can be referred to as pictures in the mind (Piaget & Inhelder, 1969) that symbolize the past experiences of the child. They are not exact copies of external objects or actions but are imitations of earlier sensory perceptions of those objects or actions. Children use these mental images to internally carry out action sequences and to remember things from the past. Others cannot observe these images, but individuals can access their own mental images if they close their eyes and picture someone they know well, like their sibling or parent. This image would resemble the person, but it would not be an exact copy of the person.

Verbal Evocation

Verbal evocation refers to the ability to use language to talk about events or actions in the past, present, or future. It can be as simple as when a child says "Daddy" after the father has gone, or as complex as recalling a past experience the child has had and telling others about it. For young children, verbal evocation is a more difficult form of representation to learn in that the signs are conventional in nature and do not resemble the things being represented. For example, the word "cow" has no resemblance to the animal. The use of these signs or words has to be acquired through interactions with others who use language. However, once acquired, language, both oral and written, is a form of representation that can be used by children to symbolize their experiences.

Learning after the Sensorimotor Stage

Once children have developed their early cognitive, language, and representational abilities, they move into more significant periods of cognitive and language development. It is at this point that the children's talk becomes a meaningful representation of their thought or of what they know, and their thought has moved completely from the sensorimotor stage to the preoperational stage. Now they are able to use perception to develop mental structures that are more complex than the earlier sensorimotor ones. While this is a major advancement, their thought is still somewhat egocentric in nature, in that the child lacks transformational reasoning. For example, a child might be able to reason that there are five chips on the table, but when the five are moved so that the configuration differs, he has to recount the chips to see how many there are.

Preoperational thought is characterized by the child's lack of reversibility, or the ability to understand that if one plus two is three, then two plus one must be three, and by centration, where the child attends to only one characteristic or aspect of a set of objects without considering other aspects of the set of objects. For example, a child watches while the teacher puts out a number of blocks in a row and then moves them closer together and asks if there are now more blocks, fewer blocks, or the same number of blocks. The preoperational child focuses on the length of the row of objects and holds that there are now fewer objects.

During this period, children construct the majority of the system of language being used by those with whom they interact on a daily basis. They do this without any kind of explicit instruction in a very short period of time (Lindfors, 1991). Between two to three years of age, children acquire the use of all but the most complex phonemes of the English language, such as l, r, s, th, sh, ch, v, and z, although the final phonemes may not be fully acquired until the child reaches four or five years of age. By the age of three they are able to conventionally speak a high percentage of the words they use. Their speaking vocabulary grows from less than 150 words to as many as 500 words and includes the use of nouns, action words, locational words, and negatives. During this period, children begin to use some contractions such as "I'm" or "don't." They are able to understand and respond to approximately 900 words and to engage in meaningful conversations with adults and other children. Children continue to develop and become more sophisticated in their use of all language functions, but most particularly the ability to use questions to gather information from others and to ask for explanations when talking with others.

From three to four years of age, children continue to improve their pronunciation abilities and are able to use most consonantal sounds with the exception of some glides, like "yittle" for "little" and voiced fricatives, like "dis" for "this" and "dat" for "that." Their sentence length grows to include four or five words per sentence, and they begin to use connecting words to form compound sentences. They are able to use contractions like "can't" and "shouldn't" and use the past tense to communicate about things that have occurred in their past. The child's vocabulary grows rapidly and consists of a speaking vocabulary of more than 1,000 words and a comprehension vocabulary of up to 2,000 words. Additionally, children increase their vocabulary by identifying new meanings for the words they have already acquired.

Children have many opportunities to hear new words when they listen to stories being read to them and as they look at the illustrations in the books to aid in their meaning making. They also begin to use a narrative-like voice to talk about their own experiences, and they start to use decontextualized language that does not assume that their listeners share the same information or perspective. However, before the age of five, children are still unable to differentiate between the object and the word for the object. For example, a child tends to believe there is only one person named Johnny because children of this age do not differentiate between the person and the name.

Children begin to show an interest in using writing instruments such as crayons or pencils to make marks on paper. Their marks begin as scribbling on paper for pure pleasure but, by three, they move to the preschematic stage in their ability to use marks as representations. This is the child's first attempt to produce a drawing that is representational. It usually consists of a person that has a circle for the head and lines for arms or legs. As this ability develops, they are better able to section the body parts so that the forms are more recognizable and complex.

Between four and five years of age, children's language ability becomes almost completely developed, so that their spoken language sounds more adult-like in terms of conversation and understandability. Their sentences range in length from six to eight words, and they continue to acquire an average of two new vocabulary words each day (Biemiller, 2005). By this stage, children's language has become completely decontextualized in that they can use a highly specific vocabulary to talk about experiences that happened at a different place at a different time. They are now able to use many different types of sentences, such as questions, affirmations, negatives, and imperatives (Lindfors, 1991) and are able to engage in conversations with other children and adults. They learn how to participate in conversations through turn taking so that only one person speaks at a time, and they begin to tell stories about events and experiences they have had. However, generally these narratives are brief and lacking in detail.

Just as the children's language matures, so does their ability to symbolize ideas and events they want to remember or share through drawing. These drawings move from the making of simple objects or people to using the drawings to tell a story or to work on a problem the child is having. Additionally, they begin to contextualize their pictures by including a blue line at the top of the page to represent the sky and a green or brown line at the bottom of the page to represent the grass or ground. They use this framework for making a variety of different pictures.

Children develop an awareness of print as they begin to recognize commercial signs like *McDonald's* and *Kmart* and as they look at the words in the books being read to them. Some children begin to use the words "scribble scrabble," a term they have constructed, to talk about the marks they put on the paper under their pictures. This provides evidence that they have differentiated drawing and writing. They also show an interest in learning to write their names and to name the letters they use as they write them.

The Adult Role in Early Learning

Children learn as they interact with significant others. They use their cries and coos to relate to the people in their environment. If we look closely at these early expressions and the methods used by adults when responding to their infants, we can identify four very important ways that adults foster early learning that can be highly successful.

1. Adults' authentic responses to the child's movement and language attempts.
2. Adults' ability to provide an authentic language model when conversing with children.
3. The willingness to accept and support whatever their child is trying to communicate or do.
4. The enjoyment and pleasure the adults evince while interacting with the child.

Responding

From the time the child is born, most adults should and do respond to the infant's actions and communications. When the baby cries, they immediately try to find ways to alleviate the cause of the cry. They are authentic in their response, in that they try to determine why the child is crying. "Are you hungry?" "Do you need your diaper changed?" They alleviate the source of discomfort and, all the while, talk to the infant in a soft, calm way. Most adults respond when they hear the infant coo or gurgle, and they talk with the child in response to the sounds they make. It is as if they were having a conversation with the infant and taking turns at talking. Adults also usually respond to the child's attempts to turn over, sit up, and crawl. This kind of responsive interaction helps build intimacy between the adults and the infant and fosters the children's interest in their environment (Burkato & Daehler, 1995).

As the infant moves into cooing and babbling, most adults continue to respond to the sounds they are making as if they were conversing with them. They do not try to correct these babbles but rather respond to them as if they make sense. These responsive conversations with infants and toddlers have been found to be up to six times more effective in promoting language learning than is reading to them (Zimmerman et al., 2009).

Soon children begin to combine sound combinations into syllable sounds that are repeated like "dada" or "mama." Because these combinations sound like "real words," adults respond to them with great pride and joy, which in turn encourages the child to continue to put sounds together to make words. Throughout the language learning period, the adults respond with smiles, hugs, and words to each step the child makes. They are excited to see how quickly and easily the child is learning to talk, and they are eager to respond to all utterances the child makes.

Early on, children begin to act on objects and to use them to satisfy their needs. They learn as they play with the objects the adults provide for them, and they learn as they touch and feel the things within their environment. Adults encourage children's cognitive development by providing the materials and opportunities for children to act on objects through pushing, pulling, and climbing.

Modeling

According to Pruden et al. (2006), infants listen to adult conversations to try to understand the conversations long before they can speak. The researchers found that, even before they are talking, children were able to learn two new words in a single interaction with the adult. This suggests the important role that modeling has in the child's early language development. Adults serve as language models even when they are conversing with others in the presence of the infant.

Adults use "motherese" to interact with their children and provide a model for the children to follow with their cooing and babbling. This kind of speech has features that attract the infants' attention. They include the use of a slower tempo, an affectionate tone, a higher pitch, and many content words. It is essential to remember that the adult continues to converse with the child even though the child does not verbally respond. Along with engaging infants in conversations, adults model their pleasure in the sounds their child is making by repeating them. They smile, clap, and use eye contact to model their pleasure when infants help pick up the toys as they name them. Additionally, adults model their enjoyment of story as they read books to the infants. By 30 months of age, the child's rate of language development has been found to be significantly related to how much the mother talks to the child during shared activities like reading books, doing household chores, or playing (Wells, 1986). Adults model language as they interact with others throughout the daily activities. The child listens while adults talk on the phone and when they answer the door. This helps the child understand the importance of learning to talk.

Accepting and Supporting

When the child makes an attempt to use language, perhaps by saying "dada," adults are highly supportive of this attempt and accept the child's use of language. They understand what the child has said and respond to the child in a way that lets the child know that they understood. For example, the child says "mama" and the mother gleefully responds, "Yes, I am your mama!" The child's early attempts are not looked on as mistakes and are not corrected but rather are supported so the child will continue to try out new ways to say things.

As the child begins to play with objects, the adult supports the play by engaging in it with the child. Lindfors (1991) refers to this kind of play interaction as "jointness." This kind of play can occur when the adult and child work as partners playing with the same object, making up conversations, or inventing and participating in a variety of interaction formats or routines like the following. The adult says "How big is Mary?" Mary holds her arms way out in front and responds "So Big."

The time families spend talking to their young children matters. Conversing with young children provides them with experiences that are important to their growth and development. The research documents that the language tools provided to children through conversation and play can contribute to a child's future success in school. Additionally, research suggests that, by one year of age, children who have a larger speaking and listening vocabulary have mothers who participate in activities such as helping, demonstrating, facilitating, pointing, and giving (Stevens, Blake, Vitale, & McDonald, 1998).

Enjoying

Children love to play, either alone or with significant others. Play provides a wonderful avenue for language learning. From birth, the child loves to play with all of the different sounds she can make. Adults participate in the play with the children, and they laugh and have a good time. Sometime they play with rhyming words together and love to play hand games like "Peek a Boo" and "Pat-a-Cake." According to Cook (2000), language play is not a trivial or insignificant activity but is important to learning, creativity, and intellectual pursuits.

As adults play with their toddlers, they are able to ask them questions like "What do you do with that?" to initiate conversation. They are also able to make comments about the objects the child is using in the play: "Oh that is a beautiful ball!" The way that adults play and interact with their children makes a decided difference in their later language growth. It has been determined that adults need to spend at least 30 minutes a day in meaningful play, talk, and listening with their infants (Ward, 2001).

English Language Learners (ELLs)

Early childhood classrooms in the United States are in a period of racial and ethnic transition. In 2008, there were 505 counties in the United States where minorities made up at least 50% of the county's youth. An additional 286 counties had minority populations of between 40 and 50% (Mather & Pollard, 2009). Many of these children are now considered second generation minorities as they are born to at least one foreign-born parent. Because of the enormous changing population patterns of the United States, an understanding of bilingual language development, biliteracy, and English language learners is essential.

Addressing dual language learners is important in all classrooms. Shared Journal combines drawing, oral, and written language, making it an ideal process for multilingual classrooms. The following offers a brief overview of bilingual language development and shows how Shared Journal is a valuable curriculum in multilingual and bilingual classrooms.

Currently, some researchers are shifting their study of bilingual children from case studies of individual children (Leopold, 1939; Ronjat, 1913) to studies of groups of children. Some are interested in whether bilingual children have two separate languages from the beginning (Genesee, Nicoladis, & Paradis, 1995) or one language system, that splits into two systems as they become involved with the second language (Volterra & Taeschner, 1978). These two lines of research are important to teachers because of children's abilities to reach milestones in language development. At the present time, most of the research (Junker & Stockman, 2002; Oller, Eilers, Urbano, & Cobo-Lewis, 1997) supports Genesee's hypotheses that children have two separate languages from birth. This line of research is important because it helps teachers to know how to approach the language learning of these children. If the single language system research is accurate, then children would mix grammatical rules, words, and phrases which would cause confusion in using either language and slow their language development in both languages. If, on the other hand, the two languages are separate, they can learn to use both languages in a bilingual manner.

Based on their hypotheses about separate language learning from the beginning, Genesee, Paradis, and Crago (2004) and others are focusing their research on code switching and code mixing. When children use code switching and code mixing, they alternate between the two languages' phrases, words, and even phonemes. According to Genesee et al. (2004), children use code switching to fill in lexical or grammatical gaps in their knowledge of language. They may code switch when they do not know a translation equivalent for the word or phrase. Second, they may code switch because they want to add emphasis or convey an emotion for what they are saying. Finally, they may use code switching to fit into their community's rules and expectations for language. This use of code switching is not unlike what English speakers do when they switch from formal English to informal or dialectal English.

Although most people are aware of the term "bilingual" when discussing children's language development, many have now become aware of the term "biliteracy." Biliteracy describes children's literate competencies in two languages that may be developed at the same time or successively (Dworin, 2002). In other words, children are able to understand and use written symbol systems and cultural tools from more than one culture. This biliteracy allows children to have a much broader understanding when reading a piece of literature because they are understanding it from two cultural perspectives. This richness in understanding should be encouraged and expanded rather than ignored because it does not fit within the Standard English language system.

English language learning is an additional kind of language learning that teachers need to consider. English language learning means that the child who has a first language other than English then learns English as a second language within the context of an English-speaking country (e.g. United States, United Kingdom, Australia). More and more children are entering United States classrooms as English language learners. When they arrive, they typically have limited or no English proficiency. Researchers (Genesee et al., 2004; Robertson & Ford, 2008; Tabors, 1997) have found that it takes five to seven years for children to achieve advanced fluency in their second language. They also point out that the children go through four to six stages (or more) as they achieve second language fluency.

Children's first stage is using their home language. They seldom use this for very long because they realize that they cannot communicate effectively with it. Next they go through a nonverbal or silent period because they are acquiring the second language receptively. This period may last from six weeks to a few months, depending on the child's age and personality. In the early production phase, children begin to speak using short words (e.g. "Please!" "Yes!") and sentences ("I don't want that."). They are imitating other English-speaking children and adults in their surroundings. During this stage, the children make numerous errors. Their major focus is still on receptive language. The fourth stage is the language production stage. It may be broken down into early production, speech emergence, and beginning fluency. At this point, the children use English more frequently, make and use longer sentences, and consider using it in social situations. Although they rely heavily on ready-made phrases (e.g. "I have that too." "I go home.") and continue to make errors because their English vocabulary is increasing, they are becoming more fluent. The last stages are intermediate fluency and advanced fluency. In these stages, the children will continue to make errors, but those errors begin to diminish. The children are able to speak fluently when discussing academic subjects and engaging in social situations. They are also able to think in English, so that they can problem solve and offer arguments in English without having to think in their first language and then translate into English.

Disposition towards English is an essential component if children are to achieve advanced fluency in English. They must see the use of the English language as meaningful. It has to meet a specific need, whether that need is social or academic. They must experience English in authentic situations so that they are motivated to put the time and effort into learning and using it. Shared Journal is a strategy that offers children the opportunity to develop positive dispositions towards using the English language. It allows children the opportunity to hear other children speak English, to participate in oral questioning, sharing, and conversations, and to write stories. It has a social component so that the English language learner has an intrinsic need to participate. If the classroom environment is culturally and developmentally appropriate, then the second language learners will have the opportunity to take risks with English by making mistakes without fear of punishment or ridicule.

Difficulties in Early Language Learning

Although all children acquire their native language at a very rapid rate, by the age of four or five there are remarkable differences in what they have acquired. Linguistic differences related to dialectal variations and social classes are acquired at a very early age. For example, there are many different variations in the communicative style for Spanish-speaking individuals. Additionally, there are many variations in the speech styles of African American individuals. Consequently, by the time some children enter preschool or kindergarten, the language ability they have acquired can be decidedly different from that of the majority of the other children. This factor can make certain kinds of prereading activities, such as phonological awareness, more challenging for preschool and kindergarten children who use language variations that differ from Standard English (Hagemann, 2001).

Socio-economic status is another factor that affects the rate of language acquisition. By four years of age, children born into higher socio-economic families have been exposed to 45 million words, while children born into lower socio-economic families will have been exposed to only 13 million words (Hart & Risley, 1999). This creates a significant difference in their vocabulary development and is usually accompanied by the use of shorter utterances and a less developed phonological system. All of this has to be considered in the preschool and kindergarten classrooms, so that these children are able to grow in their use of language.

There are some children who suffer from language disorders due to such problems as stuttering, hearing loss, mental retardation, traumatic brain injury, and autism spectrum disorder. Teachers often confuse language differences, such as those mentioned above, with language disorders. Identification of children with language disorders or delay is essential and requires the help of a variety of professionals (e.g. speech-language pathologists, audiologists). Many of these disorders are not identified until children enter preschool or kindergarten. Because these problems usually require the attention of speech therapists, teachers have the role of supporting these children's growth in their classrooms by providing social environments that encourage adult–child and child–child interactions. Strategies for using Shared Journal with children with such disorders and delays are extremely beneficial and will be addressed in a later chapter.

Summary

Young children learn through their daily interactions with significant others in their immediate environment. They learn to hear, speak, and understand the language into which they were born, and they learn to think through their interactions with the people and things in their environment. They move from sensorimotor thought to preoperational thought through a variety of interactions with people and things, and throughout this period they learn to understand and use their native language. Adults are crucial to the children in these developmental processes. This foundational understanding of how children learn is instrumental to the effectiveness of Shared Journal, which will be discussed in the next chapter.

two
The Process of Shared Journal

Shared Journal is based on the understanding that young children can learn in school in the same natural way they learned during the very early years of their life. It is an instructional practice based on the theoretical tenet that individuals construct their own knowledge (Piaget & Inhelder, 1969) and that children develop that knowledge through social interaction with others (Kamii & Randazzo, 1985). In Shared Journal, children do this through telling about events from their lives, asking and answering questions, talking with others, and reading their stories.

The basic steps in the daily Shared Journal process include the following:

1. Determining who will share.
2. Sharing the stories with classmates.
3. Learning more about the story through discussion and questioning.
4. Recording a way to remember the story through key words or titles.
5. Negotiating which story will be written in the journal.
6. Recording the selected story in the journals.
7. Reading the story with others.
8. Celebrating progress in journal entries.
9. Sharing journal entries at home.
10. Using journals as a reference.

The last three steps may be completed on a daily, weekly, or monthly basis.

Preparation for Shared Journal starts before children arrive for the first day of school and the process continues until the last day of school. There are a multitude of steps in Shared Journal, and this chapter will discuss and provide examples for the preparation for Shared Journal as well as each step in the process.

Preparation for Shared Journal

Preparing the Journals

Before implementing Shared Journal, the teacher or students must prepare the journals. Each journal consists of a page for every day of the month, and these pages are contained in a selected cover. Folders, folders with brads, or notebooks are some of the options teachers choose for the journal cover. Teachers may ask parents to send one folder for every month of the school year or teachers may provide these folders for the children. For the pages, teachers may use unlined paper for preschool and kindergarten children, partially lined paper with room for a picture for first and second grade children, and lined paper for children who are developmentally ready to write on lines and no longer have a desire or need to include pictures with their stories. Sometimes the children will draw their own lines, indicating that they would like to use lines for their writing. For younger children, the pages are inserted in the folder so that the journal opens from bottom to top in landscape format. This is helpful for younger children as they develop the concept of left to right. Their writing tends to be slightly larger and needs more room. Also, the landscape format provides more space for the children to illustrate their stories. On the outside of the folder, the child's name is written underneath the title, *My Journal*. Children may also indicate the month below their names on the journal covers. The process may begin on the first day of school or on the first day of the first full month.

Preparing the Children

Once the journals are prepared, the teacher needs to begin preparing the children for the Shared Journal process. Stories are a vital part of an early childhood curriculum. In any classroom on any given day, there are children who cannot wait to tell something that has happened in their lives. The urge to talk about an event that has personal meaning is so strong that the children will persist in engaging in conversation with the teacher or will tell their stories over and over to their peers. Children volunteer to share personal experiences or at times may show items they bring to school (Taylor & Cleveland, 1986). According to Taylor and Cleveland, children tell stories of personal events that may include a special trip or vacation, going to Hardees, getting a permanent, or going to a school pep rally. Britton (1982) stated that, when children are given the opportunity to talk about events, they form these events in language and make them an avenue to their learning process. This talk allows children to create meaning from the experiences.

Throughout the day, the teacher should always listen and interact with the children about these stories. This is usually accomplished through impromptu conversations with individuals or a small group of children. While this should be a normal occurrence in a classroom, the teacher will need to begin paying particular attention to what the children share about their lives, because these stories will be potential entries for the journal. In the unpublished study by Cleveland (1989), which focused on the influences on children's writing topics, kindergarten children shared events from their personal lives in order for their stories to be considered by their peers as topics for journal writing. Children appeared to be highly motivated and opted to tell their own stories because they wanted to be written about by their classmates.

Also, during story time or shared reading, the teacher should call attention to the authors and illustrators of books that are read. This, too, is a common instructional teaching strategy but has specific relevance to the Shared Journal process. The children need to develop an understanding that they will be the authors and illustrators of their own books—*My Journal*. This daily instruction, along with the continual interaction about experiences in the children's lives, will help them as they begin the Shared Journal process.

The Shared Journal Process

Determining Who Will Share

FIGURE 2.1 Signing Up to Share

Once the teacher is ready to begin Shared Journal, a sharing board is placed in the large group area. Poster boards, wipe-off boards, or interactive whiteboards are some possibilities for sharing boards. As children share events from their daily lives with the teacher, they talk about the possibility of sharing their stories with the class. This communication is crucial in screening for topics and determining who will share. It is important for the teacher to help children determine if their stories are appropriate for the group or if their stories are ready to be told. Sometimes children may share about a fight that occurred at home or some other subject that may be of a sensitive nature. By discussing the topic with the teacher, inappropriate subjects for sharing with the class are determined. If a sensitive topic is shared with the class, it is the responsibility of the teacher to help guide the conversation and questioning in order to assist the storyteller and the audience in their understanding of the content. Also, after talking with the teacher, children may decide that they are not ready to share a particular story. For certain reasons, they may want to wait before sharing with the group.

Once the teacher and child agree that the story needs to be included in the day's sharing, the child writes his name on the sharing board to indicate that he will share a story with the class during a large group time. The number of children who share depends on the children's stories and the time available in the teacher's schedule for sharing. It is generally best to have at least three children share their stories, but this is not required. If only two children share, the children may view sharing as a win/lose situation. With at least three children, there does not appear to be a winner and a loser. This is especially important with younger children. However, it is not always possible to have three children share stories. Some days only one child may share or there may be four equally good stories.

Sharing the Stories with Classmates

FIGURE 2.2 Sharing and Discussing a Story

The children who have signed up on the sharing board take turns sharing their stories with their classmates. When young children tell personal stories, they think the listener has the same background information that they do. They think that their thoughts are common to others and that they understand one another (Piaget, 1977). For example, John, a kindergarten child, says to his classmates, "I found a bird nest." This child assumes that the listener knows other details, which may include what a bird nest looks like, where he found it, who was with him when he found it, and what he did with it after he found it. His oral story consists of only one sentence. When children participate in the Shared Journal process, they talk about personal experiences or events with their peers. In the beginning, these stories do not contain many details but include additional story elements as time progresses.

Learning More About the Story Through Discussion and Questioning

After the child has told his story, the other children are given opportunities to ask questions. Dialogue abounds among the children, with questions and comments flowing freely. In the Branscombe and Taylor (1988) study, transcripts of children's talk during sharing time and the completion of the journal entries demonstrated the use of repetition, elaboration and questioning, details of setting, and sequence of events. The children elaborated on their own definitions so that their peers could have a better understanding of the story. Also, the children used information that they gained during peer–peer interactions in their journal entries. It is through this dialogue during the questioning that children learn what elements are important to include in their stories. This questioning helps them to know what details to include the next time they share, thus increasing story length. It is important for the teacher to keep the sharing and questioning focused and moving along in regard to the time allotted. Also, emphasis should be on the story and not on the child. This helps the children to focus on the subject and not the person as they determine the journal topic.

In examining the role of social interaction in the formation of shared meaning, researchers looked for evidence of how children interpreted and brought meaning to an event (Taylor & Cleveland, 1986). It was concluded that children share the same meanings only when they have had some experience with the topic being shared. Additionally, the shared meaning seemed to serve an important function in that children began to listen to others during the sharing time and to initiate their own questions. Because of their similar experiences, the children had a personal interest in the story, and they asked questions or made comments based on this shared experience. Their personal experience with a similar topic gave them a way to connect with the storyteller. Also, results from this study generated a conclusion concerning the role of social interaction in early literacy development. The sense of community in this classroom was very strong and may have encouraged children to help one another in their construction of writing. This cooperation was reflected in the language forms of their writing. It was concluded that the shared journal proccss facilitated the movement from egocentric thought to sociocentric thought.

Recording a Way to Remember the Story Through Key Words or Titles

After each story is shared and questions are asked, the children must select key words or a title to represent the main idea of the story on the sharing board (Figure 2.3). The teacher helps the child think about what to record by asking the student, "What was this story about?" Developmental spellings are encouraged as the child writes the words that represent the main idea of the story. The key words or titles help the children remember the story when they are negotiating and voting on the journal entry.

Negotiating which Story will be Written in the Journal

After the main ideas of the stories shared are determined, the children discuss the stories. In this discussion, the children are given an opportunity to state their opinions about the

FIGURE 2.3 Writing a Title or Key Words

story they think should be the journal entry. In addition, they give reasons why they think the story should be in the journal. The teacher may facilitate this discussion and probe for their justifications. This kind of discussion is developed over time and is dependent on the thinking and reasoning abilities of the children involved. Over time, this part of the process is vital in helping children reflect on what makes a good topic for writing. Also, children have a chance to listen to others and will begin to develop an understanding of the feelings of other children. The development of negotiation depends on the children's abilities to express their thoughts and listen to points of view from their classmates.

An important aspect of the interaction process is point of view. Through conversational exchange, children are faced with the ideas of others, and these ideas may be in conflict with their own ideas. These occasions provide children with the opportunity to think about their ideas in relation to others' perspectives (Kamii, 1985, 1989, 1990). Kamii (1989) reported that children build their knowledge through attempts to better understand the events in their lives. When children encounter differing views, they may make comments to indicate their personal ideas or they may question one another. This feedback from peers promotes critical thinking (Knipping, 1991), but it is also important in the production of texts, in that feedback encourages children to reflect and meditate together (Gordon, 1989). In this context, "meaning is negotiated through the social interactions and collaborations of the learners" (Gordon, 1989, p. 5).

According to Branscombe and Taylor (1988), Shared Journal "is an attempt to maximize opportunities for exchanging viewpoints through talk in writing-related tasks" (p. 111). This process provides children with opportunities to know the perspective of others. When children voiced differing opinions about the journal topic, they participated in a discussion and negotiation process. Through this negotiation, children heard others' points of view and possibly had to adjust their own thinking. If they wanted to reach agreement concerning the topic, they had to take the perspective of another. Also, through the discussion and negotiation process, the children were exposed to the fact that events they thought were unique to them also happened to others.

In an unpublished study by Taylor and Cleveland (1986), more support was given for the importance of discussion and negotiation in helping children develop differing points of view. This study generated a conclusion concerning the role of social interaction in early literacy development. Children spontaneously shared with each other in all aspects of the writing process, and this sharing was reflected in the language forms of their writing. The strong sense of community in this classroom encouraged the children to discuss and negotiate their writing. This cooperation was reflected in the language forms of their writing. It was concluded that the Shared Journal process might have facilitated the movement from egocentric thought to sociocentric thought.

In an unpublished study of Shared Journal, Land (1998) looked at the role of talk in kindergarten children's construction of story. Examination of the discussions and negotiations that the children used to form their hypotheses about what makes a good story revealed their conceptions about story. Their hypotheses about stories that were worthy of topic selection involved both literary conceptions of story and moral conceptions of story selection. The teacher initially stressed the importance of stories that were current, novel, and special. While the responses involving stories that were special occurred the least number of times, the children argued for current and novel stories on many occasions. Children wanted to hear stories that were happening in the present time and that were different from other stories. They did not want to hear the same stories all the time (e.g. telling over and over that someone lost a tooth).

Some hypotheses that involved literary qualities rose from the children's own spontaneous convictions about what made a good story. These hypotheses were not led by the teacher but were constructed by the children. The children decided that there were certain qualities in a story that made it appealing to them. One of these hypotheses included the idea that stories about happy, fun, or exciting events were good choices for story selection. This hypothesis was named the "happy" hypothesis. When the children employed this hypothesis, they expressed their desire to write about stories in which they thought the storytellers were happy or liked what happened to them in the stories, such as getting a new pair of shoes. Also, the children labeled a story a happy story because it was about something fun or exciting, such as having a birthday party or a new baby brother or sister.

In addition to their ideas about happy stories, the children also developed the idea that stories about something bad, sad, or tragic that happened to the story characters were worthy of consideration during topic selection. This hypothesis, constructed by the children, was called the "bad" hypothesis and was used with the same frequency as the "happy" hypothesis. For example, a story about a bicycle wreck or about going to the hospital or about the storyteller feeling sad would be considered by the children as a "bad" story and therefore deserving of their consideration when choosing a topic for the journal.

A final hypothesis that the children constructed about what made a good story was one in which the children extended the bad or tragic events in a story to even worse occurrences or they changed the story event, which may not have been tragic, into a catastrophe. This hypothesis was named the "what if" hypothesis. This hypothesis involved responses by the children that began with words like "if," "because," "because if," and "because maybe." These responses were about tragic events that the children thought could have happened to the story characters but did not. For example, a story about a tree falling in a yard became a story in which the tree fell on the house and hurt the people inside or a story about a camping trip became a story where the campers were hurt by a fox. This was a strategy the children used to make the stories even more appealing to the audience and thus increase the chances of those stories being selected as the journal topics.

Hypotheses given by the children that revealed moral conceptions of topic selection involved fairness, empathy, and popularity. In the rationales given by the children that included fairness, the children were concerned that their classmates should have an opportunity to have their story selected as the journal topic. To them, it was important that consideration be given to the person during story selection. In addition to being fair to their classmates in story selection, the children expressed empathy for their classmates' feelings when considering stories as a journal topic.

In the sharing of stories, the elements of comedy and tragedy attracted the children to want to write about these topics. The children wanted to hear stories that made them laugh and cry. They found comedies and tragedies interesting and compelling. Stories that draw an emotional response from the listener are more appealing and create more interest for the audience. The construction of the "bad" and the "what if" hypotheses parallels the effect that tragedy, both in literature and in current events, has on adults. As humans, we are compelled to attend to these tragic events. In the same way, the children are attending to these bad occurrences or are including or extending bad events in stories so others will be compelled to select these stories as journal topics. Because the children wanted to choose some stories based on fairness and empathy, they demonstrated their early abilities to see things from another child's perspective and to express what they thought were their classmates' feelings. They wanted to be fair in their story selection so their classmates would get an opportunity to have their story as the journal entry.

Voting

At the end of the discussion and negotiation time, if consensus has not been reached, the children will vote on the journal entry for the day. Voting is part of the learning process, especially for young children. They have to learn that you may only vote once, and they also have to understand that what they voted for may not be the selected topic. Because voting in society is by secret ballot, some teachers have the children close their eyes or allow older children to determine their own secret ballot process. There are times when the vote may be unanimous, and there are times when there may be a tie vote. These times pose interesting questions about how the children think this should be handled. There are times when the children will decide on the topic during the discussion and choose not to vote because they have reached a consensus. However, voting is normally a part of the daily process.

Throughout Shared Journal, the teacher serves as a facilitator. As the children develop

FIGURE 2.4 Voting for the Topic

and become more comfortable with the process, the teacher may give more active roles to the children, such as facilitating their own sharing, questioning, discussing, and voting. As the children become more independent and responsible, they assume more ownership over the process. Being active in the process provides an opportunity for the children to develop their thinking and level of reasoning.

Recording the Selected Story in the Journals

Once the journal entry is selected, children begin working in their journals. While the children are opening their journals to the daily page, the teacher may review specific details of the story so to help the children think about how they want to represent the story in their illustrations or what they may want to include in the written text. With preschool and kindergarten children, it is important for the teacher to allow time for the children to begin representing the story through the picture. The drawing is critical to help the child recreate the story and prepare for the writing of the text. With young children, the pictures may be very simple with few details. This develops as the children are encouraged to include more story elements. Also, conversations among the children during this time promote the inclusion of details in the picture and text. For example, a child may ask, "What color was your bike?" "Was it day or night when you went?" "Did you go in a car or truck?" "How many candles were on your cake?" These conversations among the children reinforce the elements of the story. While the children are working, the teacher continues to move from child to child and talk about the picture

FIGURE 2.5 **Writing in the Journal**

and possible written text for the entry. With older children, there may be less emphasis on the illustration and more focus on the written text.

In the beginning, teachers can use different methods to help young children learn how to represent the story with written text. One method is dictate, trace, and copy. Using this method, the children dictate their story as the teacher prints it on the page. Then the children are encouraged to trace or copy any part of the written text and to read it to the teacher and to other children in the classroom. Another method is to look at the child's picture and say, "Now put some writing with your picture." This encourages the use of developmental spelling as the child thinks about how to write what he is thinking. It is important that the teacher know the students' abilities so that students who are ready to experiment with the writing of the text are given that opportunity. As the children develop, writings with developmental spellings are encouraged. Progress and accomplishments are recognized and praised as the children move toward independent writing.

Using Word Books

Word books may be included in Shared Journal in order to assist the children with their writings. These books are prepared by the teacher or students and are small in size so as to be handy for student use. Word books are organized like a dictionary and have upper- and lower-case letters of the alphabet in the top right-hand corner of each page. They also allow for a more realistic and authentic strategy for assisting children with their writing.

If a child has achieved a level of writing that includes the phoneme representation for words, a word book may be utilized. After receiving a word book, a younger child and teacher will determine if a word may be included in the book. This process involves having the child look for the page where the word may be written. For example, the word ball would go on page Bb. After finding the page, the teacher or child writes the word. The child may also draw a small picture beside the word. In order to keep children from depending on the word book for writing the stories or focusing on the correctness of the spelling, they do not get to put new words in their books every day, nor may they ask for every word for their journal text. The purpose of word books is to help the children move toward conventional spelling, not stop them from writing because they do not know how to spell all of the words correctly. The use of these books and the additions of words are left to the discretion of the teacher, who should have ample knowledge of the child's level of development.

During Shared Journal, the word book can be a motivation for writing for some students. In an unpublished study (Taylor & Cleveland, 1986), a child loved his word book and was more excited about writing his journal text after he began using his book. After he finished kindergarten, his mother explained that he kept his word book in the side of his father's recliner. He wanted to have it in a safe and handy place. She said he would sit in the recliner and ponder over his book. Also, on the beginning day of first grade, he took his word book to school. He felt it was important to have it with him, and the teacher needed to see what he knew. For this child, the word book facilitated his interest in writing and was a highly valued asset.

Reading the Story with Others

FIGURE 2.6 **Conferencing with the Teacher**

Every day, the children share their journal entries with the teacher. While the children are working in their journals, the teacher moves from child to child to monitor progress. The teacher and children talk about their illustrations and read their written texts. If the child dictates the text, he and the teacher will reread this together. If the child is writing independently, he will read his text to the teacher. If the teacher does not interact with every child during the allotted journal time, he/she will need to find other times in the schedule to provide this interaction.

FIGURE 2.7 Sharing Journal Entries with Peers

In addition to sharing the journal entries with the teacher, the children are asked to share their entries with at least four of their peers. They are to read their texts to classmates. This sharing of the journal entries with peers provides opportunities for the children to develop confidence in their abilities as illustrators and authors. Also, the rereading of the texts not only helps children develop their reading skills but also allows them to build relationships with their peers as they talk about their experiences in these stories.

Celebrating Progress in Journal Entries

After the journal entries are completed for the day, the teacher may select entries to be shared with the class. For example, if the teacher wants to call attention to details, those entries with good details are selected. The child shares his entry with the class, and the teacher specifically points out how he included the details in the pictures or the text. If a child experiments for the first time with punctuation or capitalization, the teacher may choose to have the child share their entry with the class. There may be days when the teacher does not select any entries to share. Also, the teacher may ask the child to share their journal with other teachers and administrators. This is a very positive way for the

FIGURE 2.8 Celebrating Journal Entries

teacher to reinforce the child's progress and accomplishments in the journal. This sharing of the journal entries is a very effective way to motivate the children to begin to include specific elements in their entries. In hopes that their entries will be chosen for sharing with the class, the children will often include specific elements that were shared with the class in their journal entries on the following day.

Sharing Journal Entries at Home

At the end of the month, the children take the journals home to share with their parents, family, and friends. Teachers often include a letter to parents informing them of what to expect from the journal and how they may interact with their children regarding the journal entries (see Figure 2.9).

Parents continually comment on how much this sharing means to them. They love reading the monthly journals with their children, and they find that they develop a better understanding of their child's classmates. When parents come to visit in the schools, they are eager to put faces with the children whose stories they have read.

Using Journals as a Reference

The children are asked to bring their journals back to school so these books may become part of the classroom library. The journals can then be used for reading, to check the comprehension of previous stories, to calculate time related to events, and to establish bonds and similar experiences among the children. Also, children enjoy rereading these

Dear Parents,

Every day in our classroom, several students share a story about a personal experience. The experiences shared range from a trip to the beach to losing a tooth. The children ask questions and make comments about the stories that are shared. Then the students decide on which story they want to write about in their journals. Students negotiate to try to come to a consensus. If a consensus can't be reached, a vote is taken and everyone writes about the story that the majority chooses.

These stories become a history of the children in our class. I will be saving each student's monthly journal throughout the year. I will then bind their monthly journals to create one journal. Each child will take home his or her kindergarten journal at the end of the year.

In addition to the students' enjoying having a history of their class, I use the journal to help with my teaching. I've provided a list of key teaching components within Shared Journal that Darcey Caldwell compiled and I use for you to review.

Shared Journal

* Builds a sense of community
* Allows for the development of oral language skills
* Provides opportunities for children to be both the speaker and audience
* Develops the concept of story and story sequence
* Provides opportunities for children to practice "careful listening"
* Gives structured opportunities for practicing asking and answering who, what, when, where, why, and how questions
* Provides daily practice in segmenting and applying the alphabetic principle
* Provides meaningful, purposeful practice in handwriting
* Provides practice in story comprehension
* Provides daily opportunity for children to read their writing to the teacher and to classmates
* Provides practice in exchanging ideas and points of view
* Provides opportunities to solidify concept of day, week, month, etc.
* Provides opportunities to count, add, work with concepts of more and less, etc.
* Writing serves as a data source for planning small group and individual instruction

Each month I will send home the journal for you to read with your child. As you read the journal with your child, encourage him or her to elaborate about the stories shared. Complement them on their development with their writing and/or drawing. It will be exciting for all of you to observe their development throughout the year. Please try to avoid having your child "correct" spelling or other writing conventions. Remember that the journals are examples of your child's development at that particular time. We will continue to work on their use of conventions in their writing.

Please return the journal the following day so that it can become part of our classroom library and later be bound into a book for you and your child to keep. Please let me know if you have any comments or questions.

Thank you.
Angela Carr

FIGURE 2.9 Sample Letter from the Teacher

entries because they are stories from their lives. These stories are their personal experiences, and they love talking about them and sharing the many feelings they have about these stories. They reminisce about these memories and are building relationships along the way.

All monthly journals are sent home at the end of the school year. Some teachers bind them together so the children will have a history of their school year when they take the bound copy home at the end of school. Teachers often include a letter at the front of the bound journal explaining that the journal is a record of the stories from the lives of the students throughout their school year. Some teachers choose to have the students write this letter to the reader (see Figure 2.10).

Dear Reader,

We wrote this book. This book is about what happened to us and other people when we were in kindergarten. This is something special.

We all wanted to share. Some of the stories our friends shared broke our hearts and some stories made us laugh and holler. We are glad we have these stories in this book because we can read them all over again when we grow up and laugh again. We hope you enjoy our stories, too.

Sincerely,

FIGURE 2.10 Sample Letter from the Students

When the children receive the bound copy of their journal, they are amazed at the amount of their work and the progress shown in the illustrations and text. Again, they begin to go through the entries and talk about past experiences and stories they enjoyed. Also, some classes have made class books that contain the favorite journal entries for the year. The child's journal for the school year is a treasured book and one that will forever bring back those relationships, emotions, and memories.

Summary

To implement Shared Journal, there are a number of steps to be followed as outlined in this chapter. Following these steps will help the teacher make the experience more valuable for children as they advance in their learning. Teachers are encouraged to follow the steps as designed, but they may adjust the schedule or make changes to meet their individual curriculum needs.

three
Learning in the Communicative Arts

The communicative arts include the language arts of speaking, listening, reading, and writing and the visual arts of viewing, designing, creating, and producing. They are taught in the preschools, in the kindergartens, and throughout the elementary years as children learn to converse with their teachers and others, read good literature and the writings of others, write letters and stories, and draw, design, and create works of art.

Children's knowledge in the communicative arts is fostered on a daily basis as they participate in Shared Journal throughout the school year and have opportunities to engage in conversations with all of the children in the classroom. These daily opportunities provide a time and a place to express personal experiences and feelings and to listen and respond to the experiences and feelings of others. Additionally, they provide opportunities for children to draw and write about one of those shared experiences through pictures and print and to view the pictures and reread the stories their classmates have written. These daily activities promote and refine children's development and learning in communication abilities. The purpose of this chapter is to document and explain the different kinds of communicative abilities that children develop through participating in Shared Journal.

The Communicative Arts

At an early age, children communicate with others about their needs and desires. Even before they talk, they cry to express hunger, pain, or loneliness. In early childhood classrooms, teachers help children improve their ability to communicate by helping them develop the ability to make and transfer meaning through culturally understood and accepted symbolic representations. Children communicate visually and linguistically. The visual arts help children learn to express their thoughts through portrayals and develop the ability to understand the thinking of others through viewing paintings, photos, and three-dimensional artifacts. The linguistic arts help children develop not only the ability to express their thoughts through speaking and writing but also the ability to understand the thinking of others through listening and reading. The linguistic arts are first developed through speaking, listening, and attention to the visual arts and later through reading and writing.

Advanced communicative and language abilities are not just the result of learning but rather of a continuous developmental process. Learning often refers to the acquisition of completely isolated bits of information that can be recalled, such as the names of the letters and the sounds heard in a word. Development, on the other hand, is the continuous refinement, elaboration, and transformation of information through active involvement with objects and people over time. A child's communicative and language abilities build over time, based on previously acquired information. According to Lindfors (1991), "Language is inextricably entwined with our mental life—our perceiving, our remembering, our attending, our comprehending, our thinking—in short, all of our attempts to make sense of our experiences in the world" (p. 8).

Through Shared Journal, children continually develop their abilities to listen to, and make sense of, the experiences of others, to remember, think about, and communicate their own experiences to their classmates, to draw and/or write about a selected experience in their journals, and to view, read, and enjoy the ways others recorded the same experience. Additionally, they develop the ability to hold meaningful conversations with their classmates and to use a variety of different conversational styles. In a child's words, "Like today, I am going to write about Grady fell down the steps. Grady tells his story. Then his story makes us sad, so we say, 'I'm sorry that Grady fell down the step like that.' You draw like Grady holding a newspaper, and he fell down the steps. He's falling. The picture helps you remember what Grady does."

The Primary Arts

Young children enter school with considerable ability to use drawing, speaking and listening as means of interacting with significant others in their immediate environments. They have already acquired most of their culture's system of oral language and have developed a systematic way to deliver and receive meaningful messages. They have completed all of this without direct instruction, and they use this system to think about their experiences and to interact with other people. However, they still have much to learn about the variety of ways to use drawing, speaking, and listening to express their ideas and to learn from others.

Drawing

Drawing is a vital part of Shared Journal. As was mentioned in Chapter 1, it is one of the earlier symbolic forms children acquire and use to make a record of events in their lives for themselves or to share with others (Dyson, 1993; Gallas, 1994). The use of drawing as a symbol system that communicates with others helps children begin to understand writing as a symbol system with the same end. According to Piaget and Inhelder (1969), early on young children begin to understand that drawings correspond to real world events, object, and actions. This insight of a symbol–world relationship helps preschoolers begin to understand portrayals as communicative devices.

When children enter school they are able to use some forms of drawing to depict their experiences, emotions, thinking, and some of their actions (Malchiodi, 1998). Consequently, many children choose to begin their Shared Journal entries by drawing pictures that represent the people and actions of the selected story. Their pictures usually depict the aspects of the story they deem most significant and represent their understandings of the meaning of the story. Because students use drawings to represent the important aspects of the story to be remembered, they are then free to concentrate on how to symbolize their stories in print.

When Shared Journal is used on a daily basis, children's ability to use drawing to portray the story continues to improve. Their drawings usually begin in an early pictorial stage and advance to use pictures to depict the situation or the characters in the shared story. For example, children begin to devise ways to depict human figures, usually starting with a circle for the head and lines for the arms and legs. Later they begin to add more details to the figures, such as hair and clothing (Gardner, 1980; Ives & Houseworth, 1980).

Children's individual drawing schemes become more apparent by the end of the kindergarten and first grade years. At this time, they are able to recognize and name each of the objects they have drawn. By the end of first grade, baselines begin to appear in their drawings as they differentiate between the sky and the ground. In later grades, children realize that they can change their drawings to represent their feelings by distorting, shrinking, or enlarging certain items in relation to their importance.

Over the year, the teacher will continue to see progress resulting from Shared Journal. As children become more proficient in creating written texts, they begin to use their drawings more as illustrations to support the text rather than as props to help them remember the story. Gradually, children begin to experiment with different ways to illustrate their stories. They use techniques like a balloon to represent speech, frames to represent a sequence of events, and the use of sequenced illustrations throughout the text to focus on specific details of the story.

Speaking

Although young children have developed a significant ability to talk to others in many different social interactions in their immediate environments, their ability to remember, picture, and think about their experiences is far more developed than their ability to talk to their teachers and not-so-immediate peers about those thoughts and experiences. According to Lindfors (1991), this ability develops when you "involve the children as fully as possible in real communication experiences that are maximally diverse situationally" (p. 375). Consequently, when children first enter the classroom, they greet the teacher with something as simple as "I cut my finger." These early attempts to communicate with less familiar others consist of short, simple utterances that are highly contextualized and are shared with only one or two people.

As the children are encouraged to put their names on the sharing board and to tell their classmates about their experiences, they begin to learn how to speak to a group of individuals who are not of their immediate environment. For example, when the child starts out with a simple statement, such as "I cut my finger," other children encourage further communication. A child might ask, "When did you cut it?," and another might ask, "How did you cut it?" This kind of questioning helps the speaker begin to think about the different kinds of information that should be included when sharing an experience. By hearing and answering all of the who, what, when, where, why, and how questions, the speaker gradually develops the ability to move from a simple sentence to a more developed narrative account that includes a variety of information that sets the experience in time, place, and person. For example, this is a transcript of a story told in the spring by a kindergarten child who had participated in the process since the beginning of the year.

My Broken Arm

By Susan Anthony Brogan

Last Sunday, I was going across on the monkey bars, and I slipped off. I broke my arm on them. I landed on my elbow. I turned my body 110 degrees. The doctor said that I have to have two pins. I got to wear my cast 13 days. Then the doctor is going to take it off and allow me to move it a little bit. I had to have surgery. It didn't hurt cause I was asleep. I took something to make me go to sleep. They had to put me to sleep with a gas mask, I fell asleep before they had me blow up the balloon.

The bed in the hospital went up and down with buttons. My room was 100. They had a big room for me so my mama and daddy could stay too!

I stayed in the hospital 2 days. My mama and daddy took me there. I got M&M's, balloons with animals on them, and some reading books. I got a balloon and a teddy bear from the nurses. One of the doctor's gave me a doctor hat. They wouldn't let me take it home. Someone else gets to wear it. When I get 16 they'll break my arm and fix it again.

In Shared Journal, it is essential that the children are able to hear and understand the storyteller so that they can determine whether they want to choose that story as the one that will best help them remember the day. Therefore, the listeners inform the speaker if they are unable to hear or understand what is being said. "I can't hear you!" or "What did you say?" are comments and questions the children use to let the speaker know that there is a problem. This kind of social interaction helps speakers learn to clearly enunciate what they are saying and to speak at a volume that all can hear. These are important speech lessons that are learned out of necessity to the situation rather than through direct instruction.

As children begin to focus on the other children as an actual audience, they start to invent clever ways to initiate the story. For example, one young boy stood before the group and said, "You will never guess what happened to me last night!" Also, children learn how to sequence the information so that the listeners cannot always predict what they are about to hear. For example, "Last night something woke me up! I didn't know what it was. I got out of bed and looked out the window, but nothing was there." In this way, children are beginning to develop a narrative style.

Finally, through daily conversations with the class as they negotiate the story for the day's entry, children increase their speaking vocabularies. They do not learn these new words because the teacher has taught them, but rather through the social interaction that exists as children participate in meaningful conversations with their classmates.

Listening

The children who are listening to the story are encouraged to ask questions of the speaker so that they may acquire more information about the experience. During Shared Journal, children have a reason to listen and ask questions in order to gather the information they need to decide on a story. The children also know they will need to create a version of one of the stories later on, so they are further influenced to learn as much as they can during the telling of the story. Thus, Shared Journal helps listeners learn to focus on the speaker and attend to what the speaker is saying. It also helps them think of significant questions to ask that will clarify events, add detailed information, and gain a more precise understanding of the experience.

Since there are many children listening to one speaker, the listeners become skilled at taking turns when responding to the speaker with a comment or a question. Additionally, they begin to understand that they have to wait until the speaker asks for questions before they speak. They raise their hands if they have questions and wait until the speaker calls on them to speak. They learn to listen to the questions of others so that they do not repeat the same question. The speaker, rather than the teacher, controls the interactions during this time. The teacher is always present during this time and may serve as a participant in the discussion. He or she models the same kind of behaviors expected of the children and may, at times, remind others of the rules governing the questioning portion of the process.

Participating as listeners in Shared Journal helps children learn to differentiate between questions and comments. Although children often make comments about the speaker's story, their primary goal is to ask questions to glean more information pertinent to the experience being shared. Although children have learned to ask questions before they enter the classroom, they advance their ability to think about another's experience and ask questions that are relevant to that experience. They learn to use questions to gain a better understanding of the speaker's experience, to interpret what the speaker is communicating, and to remember significant aspects of the experience that are of interest to them.

Children learn to make comments that are empathetic or that express an interest in the experience being shared. For example, "I'm sorry that you got hurt!" or "I went swimming, too!" They also make negative comments that show a distrust of what is being said or a disinterest in the story. For example, "I don't think that really happened!" or "We've heard too many stories about going to Wal-Mart!" Teachers help children differentiate between comments and questions by using a table like the one shown here (see Figure 3.1).

As listeners, children have daily opportunities to ask questions about the meaningful experiences that others share. According to Lindfors (1991), most children's questions can be categorized into one of three groups: curiosity, procedural, and social-interactional. Through an informal study, she found that, as children entered the primary and intermediate grades, there was a sharp decrease in their use of curiosity and social-interactional questions and a sharp increase in procedural questions. During Shared Journal, children primarily use the curiosity and social-interactional questions. Once in a while, they ask procedural questions like, "Isn't it time to vote?" Most often, they ask questions like, "What scared you?", "Did your Daddy get mad?", "Was it fun?", "When did you go?", "What happened to your bike when you fell?"

Questions Asked	Comments Made
X X X X	X X X

FIGURE 3.1 Comments and Questions Table

Curiosity questions are vital in the development of children's abilities to think and learn about the things they want to know. They use curiosity questions to search out the information they need to better understand a particular concept or to get more details of the story. Curiosity provides the motivation for learning more about a given topic, and curiosity questions should be a vital part of the curriculum in all grades and content areas. Social-interactional questions are used to initiate, clarify, or maintain relationships with other people. Children use these kinds of questions to build and maintain friendships with others and to attempt to understand the behaviors of others. Social-interactional questions are significant in building personal relationships with others.

The Secondary Arts

The secondary arts are those that follow the development of the primary arts and are usually taught in the early childhood and elementary classrooms. They include reading, writing, imaging, and creating aesthetic artifacts. Young children enter school with some ability to use viewing but little ability to use writing and reading as systematic ways to deliver and receive meaningful messages. Some have learned how to get meaning from the pictures in books, are able to print the letters of their names, and to reread simple books that have been read to them repeatedly. However, they have much to learn about the variety of ways to use viewing, reading, and writing to express their ideas and to receive ideas from others.

Viewing

When children sit and listen to one of their classmates recall a sad or an exciting experience, they have the opportunity to view that classmate and to see the kind of impact the experience has had on him or her. When children talk about sad events, they sometimes sniffle and wipe their eyes, and when they talk about exciting events, they raise their voices and smile. The listening children notice the different emotions exhibited, and they often find it important enough to record in their entries. For example, one child wrote, "I felt sad when Jack shared about his grandpa dying, and I know how he felt because my grandpa died one time." These first-hand viewings set the stage for later, more removed forms of viewing.

When children want to read what others have written about their stories, they often flip through the journals and use the pictures to help them locate the page on which their stories are written. Thus, viewing the pictures helps them locate the stories they want to reread. Additionally, sometimes the children will dramatize selected stories and videotape the plays. These tapes are stored for viewing in the classroom library and are often used at other times for enjoyment and for gathering additional information.

Writing

As was mentioned in Chapter 1, young children's oral language learning is viewed as exciting and developmental. Children learn language through constant interaction with others in their social environments and develop language as they feel a need to use speech to accomplish a specific goal. Recent research indicates that the same is true of learning to write. Through constant interaction with teachers and classmates, children begin learning to write in ways that are exciting and developmental (Vernon & Ferreiro, 1999). When they enter school they begin to learn about the alphabet and how to use letters to write their names. Often, children do not understand the reason why they need to know the letters. Shared Journal gives children a sense of an authentic purpose for writing.

Children should always sense a real purpose for writing, and having others read whatever the child writes is a good way to communicate a purpose. There are many classroom activities that provide significant purposes for writing. One purpose for writing is that it helps us remember. For example, rereading our journals and the journals of others helps us remember events in the lives of our classmates, and project lists and duty lists help us remember things that need to be done. Other authentic purposes for writing include sharing, amusing, informing, documenting, and communicating. Authentic writing always has an intended reader, even if that reader is unknown or is not present.

Sign-in sheets provide a good example of how to demonstrate authentic purposes for writing. Teachers can use a sign-in sheet that requires all children to write their names, as best they can, when they enter the classroom. This is not the same sheet that adults use to sign them in, and whatever the children put on the sheet is used as their signatures. They then use the sign-in sheet as their attendance record. If a child forgets to sign in, the teacher can say, "It seems that Mary Sue is not here today. Does anyone know why she isn't in school?" Mary Sue has to make her presence known, and the teacher can feel certain that Mary Sue will not miss signing in again.

Shared Journal requires authentic writing that begins when a child decides that he has an experience that he is eager to share. After sharing the experience with the teacher, he is invited to put his name on the sharing board. This requires writing a signature. Children learn that it is important that others can read their signatures. Many kindergarten children do not know how to write their names and use symbols to represent their interest in sharing. However, it does not take long before all of the children know how to write their names and delight in coming up with interesting signatures. Additionally, they learn how to read the names of all of their classmates.

The next instance in Shared Journal that requires authentic writing is when the speaker has completed answering all of the questions related to the story and is ready to put something on the board that will help the children remember the story. The purpose here is not to write the whole story but to find a short concise way to capture the essence of the story. Here the children are encouraged to use letters to write the main idea of the story. For example, a child might write "gt ct" for "Got cut." This record of the story's main idea helps children remember the story when the time comes to select the story to be entered in the journal for that day.

Once the children have selected the story for the day, it is time for them to record it on their individual journal pages. However, the method they use depends on where they are in the development of the symbolic function. Early on, most kindergarten and some first grade children start their entries by drawing pictures to symbolize the story. However, when these students share their entries with the teacher, the teacher should ask them to put some writing with their pictures. At first, the children may be puzzled about what they are to do but, before long, they begin to put some print below the pictures. Then, when they share what they have put down, the teacher replies, "Please read it to me." These early suggestions by the teacher help children begin to differentiate between drawing and writing and understand that they are to use writing along with their picture so that others can read what it says. This creates an authentic purpose for learning to write.

Once children differentiate writing from drawing, they begin to develop an aware-ness of the relationship between the sounds they make when they say a word and the letters they use to write the word on paper. They begin to develop the ability to segment some sounds they hear when they say a word and eventually are able to segment all of the sounds in a word. Through this process, children develop a significant phonological skill—segmentation (Vernon & Ferreiro, 1999). They proceed through a variety of approximate stages in this development and need responses from readers to confirm or reject the hypotheses they hold about how written language works. These stages have been documented with Spanish- and English-speaking children (Ferreiro & Teberosky, 1982; Vernon, 1993).

1. Differentiating between drawing and writing
   ■ Writing squiggles are not organized as part of the picture. Children use space to separate the picture and the writing squiggles that name the picture.
2. Letter stringing
   ■ Writing becomes random strings of letters or marks that are considered substi-tute objects for the drawing that they name. Marks are becoming more alpha-betic in appearance.
3. Minimum/maximum hypothesis
   ■ Writing strings are related to words and require a minimum of at least two or three letters (number varies according to the specific language). The larger the thing being represented, the more letters it needs.
4. Syllabic hypothesis
   ■ Because of the minimum/maximum hypothesis, children begin to search for ways to segment the sounds they hear in the word. Writing is related to the number of syllabic segments children hear in the words. For some children, this is only quantitative, while others use some knowledge of the particular letters that are used to represent that sound. Initial and final consonants are often used as word boundaries.
5. Syllabic alphabetic
   ■ Because English has many monosyllabic words, and because children continue to segment the sounds they hear in the words they are writing, they begin to construct a hypothesis that calls for more than one letter for each syllable in the word. They use initial, medial and final consonants as word boundaries, and use vowels as placeholders.

6. Alphabetic hypothesis
   - As children reach this level, they have a beginning understanding of the alphabetic system but no understanding of punctuation, spacing, and other features of the written language.
7. Conventional spelling
   - Children become aware of the fact that most words have an accepted conventional spelling and begin to wonder if their words are spelled correctly.

Likewise, the stages of spelling development have also been documented with English-speaking children (Kamii & Manning, 2002).

Level 1 No knowledge of the nature of written English.
   a. Drawing a picture to represent the word
   b. Using random strings of letters with no relationship between number of letters and length of word to be written.
   c. Writing the word using a minimum quantity of letters (two) where all words written have approximately the same number of letters.
Level 2 Same as 1c, but with the first letter conventionally correct. For example, "hdn" for hamster, "but" for bubblegum, and "khi" for key.
Level 3 Still writing the correct initial consonant, but are more advanced in that (i) they vary the number of letters, using more letters for longer words, and (ii) they use conventionally correct letters for more than the initial consonants.
Level 4 Referred to as "low consonantal" in that it is almost possible to read the words, but many consonants are still missing, such as "blgm" for bubblegum.
Level 5 Referred to as "high consonantal" in that it is almost possible to read the words, and more consonants appear at this level, such as "hamstr" for hamster. Additionally, many vowels begin to appear, like the a in hamster.
Level 6 Spelling of words is almost conventional in that no consonants are missing, and most phonemes are represented.

These stages provide teachers with an understanding of what they are seeing in the children's early attempts at writing and help them converse with children in ways that promote development. Additionally, this research in two different languages supports the universality of the stages children move through as they learn how to use written language. This knowledge helps teachers know that, regardless of what languages the child knows, this method of moving them toward writing is appropriate.

Kindergarten and first-grade teachers help children develop the ability to use letters to write by conferencing with the child as he draws and begins to write. They help the children listen carefully to the sounds in each word they are attempting to put on the paper. They encourage the child to elongate the word, emphasizing each phoneme heard as they attempt to write it. They ask the child how he might write that sound, or they ask the child how many sounds he hears in the word and write that number of blanks for him to use to write the sounds he heard. Soon, children accept the responsibility of listening to and differentiating the sounds for the words they are writing.

By the end of the kindergarten year, most children who have participated in Shared Journal on a daily basis have learned to spell at the Ferreiro and Teberosky Level 6 or at the Kamii and Manning Level 5 (Branscombe & Taylor, 1996, 1988). Once this understanding of how to write has developed, the teacher's attention can focus more on the compositional aspects of children's writing. These include different kinds of techniques they can use in their stories, such as the use of dialogue, quotes, figurative language, and paraphrasing.

Children's ability to develop their written narrative follows their ability to develop oral narratives. As children respond to the questions of their listeners in the development of their oral stories, so too do they develop their written stories by having the teacher and other children respond to the stories they have written. This is why it is essential that each child's story is read every day by the teacher and at least three or four of the classmates in the room.

Linguistically, Shared Journal promotes the use of the transactional voice rather than the expressive voice used in most other journal approaches. Through this voice the children learn to use a number of language constructions that usually do not appear in early expressive writing. These include the use of third person singular and plural, third person pronouns, first person plural forms, and demonstrative pronouns. Additionally, it promotes the use of compound sentences and assorted punctuation marks (Taylor & Cleveland, 1986).

Teachers conduct conferences with children about their journal entries and raise questions to help them learn more about the compositional aspects of writing. The following literary qualities outline is designed to help teachers get "inside the student's head." This, in turn, helps them determine what the student is trying to portray and the strategies the student has available to communicate that portrayal in writing. Thus, the teacher is able to use what the student knows as the instructional starting point to advance her writing ability. The outline offers the teacher suggestions for conferencing with the children regarding the compositional qualities of their writing. While each section adds a different dimension to the discussion, the first three focus on the most significant qualities to guide the child's writing.

1. **Literary qualities**
   - Meaning—What is the content, story, or purpose for the writing?
   - Does the piece move you in some way—make you laugh, cry, chuckle, or evoke a memory?
   - Is there a use of literary conventions such as figurative language, metaphor, or pun?
   - Does the piece demonstrate a specific genre?
   - Does the writer use an individual voice?
2. **Organizational qualities**
   - Does the writer speak with authority?
   - Does the piece hold together? Does the writer use cohesive strategies related to genre?
   - Does the piece have an opening, middle, and end?
   - Does the piece use unusual organizational strategies, such as foreshadowing or flashbacks?
   - Does the piece develop? Is it focused, complete, and does it have structure?
3. **Language Qualities**
   - Does the writer use clear, simple, and effective phrasing?
   - Does the writer make effective use of sentence combining?

- Does the writer select effective vocabulary?
- Does the use of language clarify and simplify the content and not draw attention to itself?

4. **Writing Conventions**
   - Does the writer use genre-specific conventions, such as he and she said dialogues in stories, first person in essays?
   - After editing, is the piece conventionally punctuated?
   - After editing, is the piece conventionally spelled?
   - After editing, is the handwriting acceptable?

5. **Writing Attitudes**
   - Does the writer like the piece?
   - Does the writer take risks and experiment with the writing?
   - Does the writer take pride in reading the piece?
   - Does the writer compare the piece to other writings?

Through Shared Journal, children learn how to write in meaningful ways. They learn how to compose interesting stories based on real experiences that others love to read and enjoy. This is partially due to the fact that they know that the teacher and several of their classmates will read everything they write.

Reading

In Shared Journal, writing development precedes reading development in terms of the ability to perceive print as a meaningful symbolic representation. However, because the teacher and their classmates read what each child has written each day, children are also learning to enjoy reading what others have written. The children are always eager to see how others have written their stories and to read the many versions of the story they have told. They are also eager to compare the pictures others have drawn for the story they shared. As children read these stories on a daily basis, they are able to observe the strategies others use in their writings, and they model those strategies in subsequent writings. In other words, through reading others' stories, they learn how to write better stories.

When children engage with books, their level of interest is in the story rather than in isolated words (Clay, 1997). Because they read stories in the journals and because they know about the story before they read it, they learn to read the journals in a very short period of time. The reading of the journals motivates the children to read other stories. When children learn to read in this way, they love to read and are highly motivated to learn to read.

Teachers use specific strategies to help children read the entries of others during sharing time. They create an atmosphere where children listen to each other during sharing time and where children talk to each other after reading their stories. These strategies include providing a place where children can go to read the stories written by others together. They provide oral language activities that focus on the words, concepts, and sentence patterns children have used in their stories. For example, when they have written about someone's lost tooth, the teacher might ask the children to identify all the words they find in others' journals that tell how the student felt when her tooth was pulled. They also engage students in activities that increase their understandings and use of the conventions, mechanics, and rhythms of written English found in children's stories.

Summary

Shared Journal provides daily opportunities for children to develop all areas of the communicative arts. The children view all aspects of the communicative arts as purposeful and relevant to their lives. It helps them make sense of and communicate their experiences and the experiences of others. Additionally, it allows them opportunities to view, read, and enjoy the way others recorded the same experiences.

four
The Reading/ Writing Connection

Quality experiences in the constructive processes of reading and writing are essential to the development of literacy. Shared Journal provides the ideal quality experience where children engage in and naturally develop their reading and writing. Research indicates that readers and writers operate from a base of "shared thinking" and that skill in these areas develops together (Fitzgerald & Shanahan, 2000; Langer, 1992; McCarthey & Raphael, 1992). The writer and the reader employ correlated mental processes in the construction of meaning, as the writer attempts to create meaning through a clear text, while the reader attempts to extract meaning from the text (Vacca & Vacca, 2002). As children prepare for reading and writing, they participate in common behaviors. Both readers and writers activate prior knowledge about subject matter related to text. Readers set a purpose for reading while writers set a purpose for composing. Readers and writers spark interest and utilize the process of constructing mental images regarding text. Writers give information, share ideas, and seek to convey meaning through text. Readers seek information and ideas and attempt to gain meaning from text. Active engagement in writing provides cognitive support for the skill of reading and enhances reading development. As writing improves through daily communicative use, reading is enhanced (Goodman & Goodman, 1983). When young children have the opportunity to write, they learn to read with greater ease. Current reading research focuses largely on the five "Big Ideas" of reading instruction: phonemic awareness, phonics, oral language/vocabulary, fluency, and comprehension. This chapter will document the ways that writing, in the context of Shared Journal, facilitates active participation and growth in each of these areas as well as other areas that are central to the process of becoming a skilled reader. In this chapter, reading coach Allyson Martin details how Shared Journal promotes literacy development in children.

Phonemic Awareness

Phonemic awareness is defined as "the ability to notice, think about, and work with the individual sounds in spoken words" (Armbruster, Lehr, & Osborn, 2001, p. 2). Researchers seem to agree on the importance of phonemic awareness for reading development. Most research has documented a positive relationship between phonemic awareness and progress in reading (Goswami, 2005). The most common cause of difficulty in children's acquisition of early word reading skills is their weakness in processing the phonological features of language (Liberman, Shankweiler, & Liberman, 1989). This finding about reading difficulties has been significant in changing how we approach the teaching of reading. Children at risk of reading failure are now able to be identified before reading instruction begins (Lundberg, Frost, & Peterson, 1988; Torgesen, 1998; Wagner et al., 1997). Other researchers have concluded that a causal relationship exists between phonemic awareness and progress in early reading (Adams, Foorman, Lundberg, & Beeler 1998a, 1998b; Stanovich 1993). Teachers who understand the importance of phonemic awareness to reading development seek to implement classroom practices that foster development in this area. Shared Journal provides an invaluable instructional strategy for meeting this need.

The focus of writing in Shared Journal is to record the story so that it can be remembered and revisited. This creates an authentic purpose for writing and a natural avenue for the development of phonemic awareness. During the writing phase of the Shared Journal process, children use their knowledge of our system of writing, as well as their knowledge of the relationship between spoken and written language, as they analyze their own speech in an effort to record the story in written form. As children analyze their own speech, they become better able to differentiate phonemes. When observing children in the act of writing, you can hear the process occurring as they repeat words they are attempting to write in an effort to stretch the sounds of the word and record them accurately.

Careful observation of children's journal stories reveals much about their level of phonemic awareness (Kamii & Manning, 2002). As children read their stories to peers and the teacher, they receive feedback that may confirm or challenge their thinking about their representations of spoken language. Journal conferencing offers the teacher an opportunity to analyze speech sounds in order to facilitate the development of phonemic awareness. The teacher may ask a student to say a word slowly, stretching the sounds in the word in an effort to have the child record sounds that are missing from their writing. The teacher may also use Shared Journal entries as a data source for planning individual or small group instruction to enhance phonemic awareness. For example, as the teacher observes in the journal writing that several children are having difficulty with hearing and representing final consonant sounds in words, small group mini-lessons can be planned that focus on this particular skill. The child's writing in Shared Journal can be analyzed in order to determine developmental stage, level of phonemic awareness, and progress in spelling. (See Chapter 11.)

Phonics

Research has shown that knowledge of letters, spelling patterns, and words, as well as their phonological uses, are necessary for reading acquisition. Therefore, good phonics instruction needs to include strategies that help children develop awareness of spellings and their relations to pronunciations (Adams, 1990). "Writing reveals the taking apart and building up potential of the code to young children" (Clay, 1998, p. 131). It highlights letter forms, letter sequences, letter clusters, and their relationship to letter sounds.

When children participate in Shared Journal, they analyze their speech and attempt to put the journal story on paper; a need to know the alphabetic principle becomes evident. Teachers can utilize writing in Shared Journal to facilitate understanding of the alphabetic system. Children are encouraged to use environmental print, books, etc., as references to aid in their attempts at spelling. Teachers may also have alphabet sheets in the journal that depict the letters of the alphabet with a picture that begins with each letter. These sheets can be used as references for letter/sound relationships as a child stretches a word and attempts to write it using developmental spelling.

The use of developmental spelling during the writing process leads to better word recognition and better spelling ability. As children listen to the story shared orally, record the story in written form, and then read the story to the teacher and their peers, they have explicit evidence that the process of encoding speech can be reversed as they decode the words they have written. Daily engagement in this process helps children to recognize the connection between speaking and listening and writing and reading. During journal conferencing, the teacher may provide more explicit instruction in application of the alphabetic principle using corrective feedback to solidify the child's understanding of specific letter/sound relationships, letter forms, letter sequences, and letter clusters. The writing again becomes a data source for planning individual or small group phonics instruction. As children read and reread their stories to peers and to the teacher, they practice skills in decoding what they have written. They often recognize the need for additional letters in words they have written or for corrections in letter/sound relationships they have represented.

Participating in Shared Journal allows for meaningful practice and application of phonics skills for real purposes and audiences. It requires that children utilize the letter/sound relationships they know and creates a need to acquire new knowledge of letter/sound relationships required to constructing meaningful text. In Shared Journal, children are able to recognize phonetic word features that are similar, as they naturally occur in authentic text. Through careful analysis of the child's writing, the teacher is able to determine when to introduce the conventional spelling for a word. When children consistently demonstrate the conventional spellings for some common, regularly occurring words such as *the*, *and*, etc., and when their temporary spellings reveal that they are thinking about the visual appearance of a word, as evidenced by the use of spelling patterns, vowels represented in all syllables, vowel digraph patterns, use of the e-marker, and/or use of common letter sequences ("youse" for use, "egul" for eagle, "tule" for tool), age-appropriate conventional spellings can be introduced. Teachers can provide children with a "word book" to record the conventional spellings they are learning and utilizing in their journal writing (as discussed in Chapter 2). The writing and utilization of these words in the journal story aids in the development of a sight vocabulary which is necessary for fluent reading. "Instant" words, such as the "Dolch" sight words, naturally occur over and over again in the journal stories and are written, and therefore read and reread, within the authentic purpose of sharing meaning.

Oral Language and Vocabulary

Oral language development is significant in the development of reading. Conversations are beneficial to children when they talk about familiar things, because this gives them meaningful opportunities to experiment with ways of expressing themselves (Clay, 1991). Oral language is the foundation on which reading is built, and it continues to serve this role as children develop as readers (Hiebert, Pearson, Taylor, Richardson, & Paris, 1998) For young children, oral language is a major tool of learning and is correlated with later reading achievement. Shared Journal provides children with daily opportunities to engage in oral communication of their ideas to others. As children share their stories with others and ask questions to clarify ideas, the system of language comes alive and develops as learners build meaning.

The interaction between storyteller and audience continues through the writing process and the social interactions that occur during the writing of the journal story. Children can be heard asking clarifying questions as they rethink the sequence and details of the story and discuss their writing with their peers and the teacher. When children are highly social, sharing their reading and writing frequently, they are likely to be active, interested readers (Baker, Dreher, & Guthrie, 2000). The act of conveying what was presented orally in written form gives the child an awareness of author and an insight into the intentions of a writer. This is the beginning of children's ability to take a critical literacy stance (Hall & Piazza, 2008).

Research indicates that a reader's general vocabulary is the single best predictor of how well that reader can comprehend text (Anderson & Freebody, 1981). It also reveals that children learn the meanings of most words indirectly, through everyday experiences with oral and written language. Repeated exposure to vocabulary in many contexts aids word learning. Children actively engaged in Shared Journal have a myriad of experiences with new words in the contexts of listening, speaking, writing, and reading. As children listen to their peers tell personal stories, they are exposed to new vocabulary. The questioning phase of the Shared Journal process allows children the opportunity to clarify meaning and to use new vocabulary in the context of speaking. The act of writing the story necessitates the use of new vocabulary in order to convey meaning. The utilization of new vocabulary in the writing of the story demonstrates a move from receptive vocabulary to the expressive vocabulary of the child.

In Shared Journal, the writing is focused on conveying the story meaning through print. Because the focus is on getting the message down on paper rather than correctness of spelling, children are freed to write new vocabulary words utilizing developmental spellings. Many of these words would otherwise be out of the realm of their writing possibility if conventional spelling was a requirement. New and interesting words appear in the child's writing that have been encountered in the context of reading stories, listening to others read, or engaging in conversations. Teachers celebrate the use of these words in Shared Journal celebrations. This provides an opportunity for new vocabulary to be introduced to the class from the natural occurrence of the word in the child's writing. The Shared Journal celebration is motivating for children and encourages others to utilize new and interesting words in their own writings.

Fluency

There is a strong relationship between fluency in reading and comprehension. In light of current research, fluency is defined as a developmental process that is shaped and influenced by all linguistic systems that give us knowledge about words (Wolf, 2009). One aspect of reading fluency is automatic recognition of words in text. When children represent a shared story through writing, they pay close attention to how words look. This helps to build knowledge of a variety of words and word structures and leads to more rapid recognition of words in reading. Words are consistently read faster when they occur in a meaningful context such as the Shared Journal story. Repeated readings of a familiar text enhance fluency. In Shared Journal, children read their stories to the teacher and to their peers. The teacher also sends the journal home each month so that the child can read, discuss, and share their stories with family members. This repeated reading allows the student to move from a focus on decoding the words they have written to a focus on a fluent rendering of their text, including phrasing and prosody.

Comprehension

Comprehension is the heart of reading. It is the interaction of the reader with text in order to gain meaning. Writing in the Shared Journal facilitates the development of comprehension and the practice of comprehension strategies. As children attempt to record the story, they engage in monitoring of the text as they read and reread what they are writing in an effort to ensure that meaning is conveyed. Attention is given to the sequence of the story and to accurately representing the main idea. Children are encouraged to include supporting details as they represent the who, what, when, where, why, and how of the story in written form.

When children write, they spend time thinking about the story as they attempt to categorize and structure their ideas. Teachers encourage children to write descriptively in representing the journal story, using details and descriptions so that their words "paint a picture" for the reader. The use of description ties directly to the ability to develop mental images, a comprehension strategy (Zimmerman & Hutchins, 2003).

As children record personal events shared from the lives of their classmates, they are able to connect with the story and the text they are writing in highly personal ways. Children may include statements that describe these personal connections in their writing: "I remember how I felt when ..." or "I know how Mary feels because I remember when that happened to me ..." Teachers can facilitate thinking about text-to-self connections by the questions they ask when conferencing with a child about the substance of the writing. Questions such as "Has this ever happened to you?", "How did it make you feel?", and "How do you think Mary felt when she couldn't find her dog?", focus on the content of the writing and foster the child's thoughtful introspection about the events recorded in the journal. The text connections that are fostered during Shared Journal transfer to the process of reading other texts and contribute to reading comprehension. Teaching children to connect to text means that they are better able to understand what they are reading (Harvey & Goudvis, 2000).

Children's awareness of print conventions is related to measures of reading ability. Writing in Shared Journal provides a natural way for print conventions to be learned in the context of authentic reading and writing. As children engage in writing, the teacher guides learning based on the needs of the individual child. Conventions of print, such as directionality and return sweep, text features, such as use of capitalization and meaningful punctuation, and text concepts, such as word boundaries and a one-to-one match between the spoken word and the written word, can all be addressed in the composition of the Shared Journal story. Knowledge of print conventions introduced or encountered in the context of shared or guided reading lessons can be reinforced and practiced in the process of writing the journal story.

Summary

Reading and writing are intimately connected processes. Often, the first pieces of text that children are able to read are their own writings. Participation in the daily Shared Journal process allows the natural interaction and integration of reading and writing for an authentic purpose. This interaction fosters growth in the development of phonemic awareness, phonics, oral language/vocabulary, fluency, and comprehension. When children are engaged in recording the Shared Journal story through writing, they are learning to read.

five
Developing the Narrative Voice

Although teachers intuitively view personal narrative as a foundation for advancing from oracy to literacy (Phillips, 1999), they seldom think about how children develop their narrative ability or the kinds of narratives children use. Furthermore, they seldom consider whether narratives are a sophisticated form of play and social interaction that children use to make sense of print. Because many teachers are aware of the importance of children's narratives, they provide opportunities for children to tell stories in their classrooms. As a result, children begin to explore and develop their narrative voice. They also experiment with ways of using their narrative voice to make their stories credible. When teachers begin to question how children are developing their storytelling abilities, they realize that children are actively constructing ways to make listeners attend to their stories. Shared Journal is a specific strategy that teachers can use to help children develop their storytelling abilities. It provides children with the opportunity to develop and use narrative voice as they share stories from their lives. This chapter documents how children's opportunities for social interaction and sharing oral and written narratives during Shared Journal help them begin to develop that narrative voice. It explains how children hypothesize about what makes a credible story that their classmates and friends will value and enjoy.

The construction of narrative voice is essential for listeners and readers of nonfiction and fiction so that they can determine whether the source of the story is trustworthy and the story itself is newsworthy (Norrick, 2004). In addition, the construction of narrative voice is necessary for the storyteller to develop the ability to keep the audience engaged and entertained. In order to accomplish this, the storyteller plays with a myriad of literary tools (e.g. flashbacks and surprise endings) to shape and sequence events of the story. As a result of the process, they move from talking about their personal experiences to shaping those experiences into personal narratives and then, at times, fictionalizing those narratives so that they have significant literary merit.

Narrative and narration include the use of oral and/or written language to retell past events and describe feelings during those events. The events within the narratives are usually sequenced in chronological order. These narratives are cultural tools that new members of the culture use to interact with the members of their social world (Branscombe & Taylor, 2000). As children explore the use of narratives, they use personal narratives which are retellings of a past event, either experienced by the narrator or someone the narrator knows, and fictional narratives, which are imaginary narrations that are from some published source or created by the speaker or writer (McCabe & Bliss, 2003).

The daily use of Shared Journal helps children develop their narrative abilities and move from statements that merely state and list events or actions to stories that shape those events or actions into literature. Furthermore, it helps children move from using their culture and its story structure as a basis for their decisions about the story (Kuntay & Ervin-Tripp, 1997) to becoming narrators who purposefully arrange and organize the events and actions to create a written, discursive presentation (Bal, 2004) that has more universality and is believable. In order to understand the children's movement from storytellers of personal experiences to narrators of stories from Shared Journal, a brief discussion of the role of narrator and narrative voice is necessary.

The Role of Narrator and Narrative Voice

Ultimately, the narrator's job is to have the audience (i.e. listeners and readers) feel that the narration is just for them. It is re-presenting the events and narrator's feelings during those events so that the narrator can connect to the audience's feelings recalled from experiencing similar events. The narrator wants the re-presenting to "verbally or textually hypnotize" the audience through the use of rhyme, alliteration, assonance, and all of the subtleties of rhythm. This re-presenting allows the audience to join the narrator as they go beyond the here-and-now and explore possible new worlds (Bruner, 1984). This can only happen if the audience and narrator have set up "networks of agreement" as to what is sad, violent, happy, funny, or truthful (Hayakaw, 1941, p. 189). These agreements allow the narrator to focus on the art of the telling as well as evoking feelings in the audience (Britsch, 1992).

Shared Journal offers children the opportunity to begin to construct a narrative voice through their retelling of stories in their own words in such a way that the stories are authentic, meaningful, powerful, and dynamic. Research into Shared Journal (Branscombe, 1991; Branscombe & Taylor, 2000, 1996, 1988) documents that children's construction of voice involves all of these components and more. This construction of voice is a step in the process of helping children develop an awareness of, and need to be part of, their culture and its language. The process allows them to organize "a psychological and social self" in relation to that culture. It occurs on two levels—social interaction and psychological reflection, with intention or meaning making being an essential component in the process (Vygotsky, 1976). It is how they make sense of the cultural importance of events such as "All of Nathan's toys and his trailer steps floated away last night when the tornado came." For many readers, this story describes a weather event. For children who live in Nathan's culture—a poor, rural community of manufactured home (e.g. trailers or mobile homes) neighborhoods—this story reflects their knowledge that the steps to a trailer are essential for entry into that home. They know that often trailers are not repaired when damaged because of the lack of money and insurance. They also know the importance of the loss of the child's toys, as those are seldom replaced.

Children's narrative voice is the speaking and/or writing persona that they choose to use to extend those retellings of personal experiences through words. Because the persona involves the individual's sense of who they are, the narrative voice reflects the children's history, economic backgrounds, emotions, reasoning abilities, and cultural realities (Phillips, 1999; Walsh, 1991). The following story shared by Gwen exemplifies this.

The Moving Day

They are moving my house today. They're using a big truck. You just hook the house up to the truck and go. It's a trailer. They've already got the front porch down. My mama had to take all the stuff out of her cabinets. We boxed the dishes. I like my new place.

Unlike children whose homes are apartments, condos, or freestanding houses with yards, Gwen's home is a manufactured home in a trailer park. Because of the mobile nature of her home, it can be moved from one location to another. This influences her understanding of homes and creates a cultural reality and history that is different from children who live in apartments or freestanding houses.

Just as with their oral voice, children's construction of their written voice develops over time, requires perspective taking and reciprocity, considers credibility, and engages the imagination so that they build their narrative persona which orchestrates their words and shares their feelings. Through orally sharing their experiences, providing additional details by answering questions that clarify those experiences, and then writing about them, the children refine their written narrative voice so that it pulls others into their stories (e.g. procedure for the Shared Journal process). This multidimensional construct helps children build the relationships necessary to have faith in "the reality of words that come in books studied in schools" (Elbow, 1998, p. 74), a precondition for taking words seriously.

In order to build the narrative voice in writing, children experiment with constructing and coordinating the authority they need over words, their information, their emotions, and the action or events those represent. They build awareness that static objects (letters and words) can represent action. Because of this, they come to know that the letters, words, or stories in a book can be produced by them to convey their own life's actions and events. In children's writings, this appears early with one or more of the following: scribbles, letter strings, picture labeling, word collections, word lists, partial images, themes, imitation of the teacher's writing, copying print in the room, summarized stories, general statements about what children have written or drawn, and written pieces of events that seemingly lack logical order.

At first, this authority may be exhibited with a statement that names one past event which is written in scribbles with "ball-and-stick," pictures. As they continue to explore this authority over experiences in their lives, they may try as many as eight general structures for personal narratives (e.g. one-event narratives, two-event narratives, miscellaneous narratives, leap-frog narratives, chronological narratives, end-at-the-high-point narratives, and classic narratives) (McCabe & Rollins, 1994). (Chapter 11 discusses these narrative structures in more detail.)

Over time, children add additional events and details about those events and are able to group their words into significant collections or patterns of meaning for themselves and others. For example, after several months of Shared Journal sharing, Angel wrote the following story, "I went to Six Flags and Stone Mountain and the beach. I couldn't go to Stick River because it was too full. It was fun." At this point in her development of narrative voice, Angel provides a list of events, sequences those events, links them and adds the comment that she had fun. It documents Angel's growth from offering one event and expecting other children to be aware of the entire story to offering three events, her reason for not engaging in another event, and her feelings about the trip. It also demonstrates a step that is involved in developing narrative structures.

As children develop their use of narrative voice, they apply their authority and control over words through the use of the spectator role (Britton, 1982). The spectator role allows them to order, shape, and reshape their experiences in writing so that they make meaning out of the seeming mysteries of the experiences and the environment in which the experiences occurred.

The spectator role allows children to use their voice to transform the everyday events of their lives into artistic experiences that they are then impelled to have others hear and/ or read. Through that hearing or reading, they hope that others will appreciate the experience by sharing the same feelings and meaning that they have. If they can make this happen, they will have helped others share these same feelings and meanings, which will validate and lend respect to their lives and the life of their community. This is exemplified by Ned's poem, which was his writing about another child's sharing of her love of gardening in the spring.

> **Ned's Poem**
> *I love the sounds of spring*
> *Because the birds sing*
> *And*
> *But*
> *The sun shines*

Ned wrote the poem spontaneously to experiment with presenting his emotions (love of spring) as symbols and images. He needed language to create the relationships (between symbols, emotions, images, and experience) and make the connections ("because," "and," "but") of the sounds and images of spring. This kind of experimentation and perspective taking are Ned's efforts to describe and organize action (Barthes in Bal, 2004; Piaget, 1962/1976).

Stages in Constructing Narrative Voice

Personal Expectations for Story

Children are born into a world of storytelling. Older language users tell stories from their own lives as well as the lives of the children. Children as young as two attempt to offer stories (Stadler & Ward, 2005). Around three or four years of age, children begin telling stories that focus on themselves and that older language learners can recognize as stories (Nicolopoulou, 1997; Nicolopoulou, McDowell, & Brockmeyer, 2006; Pellegrini & Galda, 1988). Over time and through repeated conversations about and telling of their stories, they move from this focus on hearing themselves talk to an awareness that their stories can have an impact on others. As this occurs, they begin to understand that what can happen to them and their world could happen to others. By the time they are five or six years of age, their stories reflect this interest in others. John's story about Ned exemplifies this.

> We helped Ned have Easter, cuz they [Department of Human Resources] called us and said he wasn't going to have Easter. We went to the store and bought him some. We picked him up and then he spent the night with us Friday night. The next day he helped us color Easter eggs. Then it was time for him to go home, and we gave him Easter. Now he don't live where he was anymore. He's gonna come back some day. I said goodbye to him, cuz he's my friend.

Movement from the focus on self to others occurs over time, involves several phases, and is specific to the individual child and his or her experiences. It is a highly complex task as it uses decontextualized narratives that are understood without pictures or texts (Cazden, 2001; Peregoy & Boyle, 2005). At first, children either offer a one-word sharing (e.g. "Zoo") or simple statements during sharing ("I got a new dress"). As they continue to share, they learn to offer loose collections of thought that seem more like streams of consciousness than an effort to communicate (e.g. "T-shirt, shoes, my doll"). Next, children experiment with various ways to find words that match actions and events and get the events in chronological order. For example, "Mathew is hitting and Jeremy is throwing the ball." They even construct rules that help them accomplish these two goals. It is within the need to be more specific that children begin to realize that finding words and ordering them to match the event is not enough.

Once children feel confident telling their stories with some degree of ordering of events, they realize that they want someone to hear and read what they have told or written—to care about their human experience as much as they do. At this point, children begin to watch to see the effect their words have on the readers or listeners (Elbow, 1998) and then reflect on their reactions as well as the words that caused those reactions. They learn that words carry meaning that allows someone else to take that text and hear their story. The power of this knowledge focuses children's desire to get the reader to hear and read their words. At this point, they know the relationship of reciprocity in writing and reading in such a way that they can construct the dual relationship of "readers make writers" and "writers make readers." As children are experimenting with this new knowledge, they will write Shared Journal entries like Betsy's story.

> We went to the gym and had races. Did you win?
> It was kinda fun for me. We won, [beat] Mrs. Sharman's room.
> I bet Mrs. Terrell was proud of us. Nathaniel won first Place.
> How would you feel if you won first place?

In this sharing, Betsy attempts to make sure she has engaged the audience and had them understand her by involving them through questions. In addition, she uses a historical generalization ("We went to the gym and had races"), which suggests that there were stories before this one. She also uses more of a dramatic order than a chronological order. She chooses to end her story with a question ("How would you feel if you won first place?"), which suggests that she wants her readers to recall the feelings of a time when they won first place or imagine the feelings that they might have if they won. This effort to collaborate with the readers around the story is a very different voice from one that offers a list of events in chronological order and/or reports the events in a who, what, when, where pattern. Betsy's story suggests that she wants an audience which is listening to her words and reading her sentences to share the meaning of her story.

As children develop their narrative voices, many use the same kind of constructions in their writing as they do in their oral sharing. They do this as they build awareness of the duality of the audience and writers' roles. Some writers use Shared Journal to experiment with other strategies to get their audiences involved with their stories. A few copy from the teacher's text so that they can claim the authority an adult has with words. Others add more detail to their pictures and/or more words to their texts, while some copy from peers, word walls, books, or charts. Some children team up to write and play with their stories. In one classroom, the children often turned their writing into word play. On one occasion, their classmate, Clarissa, shared about azaleas. They used their questions about spelling azaleas to make a song ("azalea, a do-do, a do-do, azalea, azalea, a do-do . . .").

All children test out strategies to move from their earlier one- or two-dimensional narrative voices to their multidimensional voices. After children begin trying the narrator's voice, they begin to think about their own worlds and the expectations of those within their worlds (e.g. Mama's rules, Daddy's rules, credible stories, telling a lie, and so on). They puzzle over how their worlds fit into their narratives.

Community's Expectations of Story

When children begin to use Shared Journal stories to reach out to their audience, they follow their community's expectations for their stories. The community may be their classroom community, their family, or their neighborhood communities. For example, one child believed that he needed to share and write about "terrible stuff." He hypothesized this based on hearing other classmates share heartbreaking or sad stories that were selected for inclusion in the journals. He explained, "I vote about terrible stuff happen and good stuff happen. When I say terrible stuff, I mean bad stuff. You got to think in your mind. You've got to figure out what bad. Then you vote and write." Another child, Zena, shared a similar reason for selecting a story when she explained why the class needed to write about Bill's story.

> Bill was happy to see his little brother [after having to be hospitalized] . . . because he was happy to see his brother, and that's the story we need to vote on because he want to see his brother sometime, and he have to see him today. This is the lucky day to see him. That's the . . . Bill the story that we need to vote on because he was happy to see his brother.

Children often view birthday parties, shopping trips, being injured, getting over an illness, and experiencing natural disasters, such as tornadoes, as topics worthy of sharing (Land, 1998).

The children in one Shared Journal research study (Branscombe & Taylor, 2000) exemplified the rule for following the expectations of the listeners and readers regarding what makes a good story. The children were from a community that was similar to the Roadville children in Heath's (2006) research. Just as with the Roadville children, these children measured a story's value by the narrator's ability to match the oral or written version with the actual event. Chad, a Caucasian child who was similar to the Roadville children, used Shared Journal to champion these expectations.

Branscombe and Taylor (2000) described Chad's monitoring of the group's use of the community's behaviors and rules for making stories. During Shared Journal, if a child told about a death in the family, Chad responded with statements like, "You always cry when people die." When Scrap told about the wedding he attended, Chad wanted to know if the bride and groom had danced and kissed "cause that's what they do at weddings." When Carrie Elizabeth told about her two-year-old brother cussing ("I'm going to boot you!") at day care, Chad responded, "Ohhh! You don't laugh when people say stuff like that. He could get in trouble a lot for cussing."

Chad valued and upheld the rule of truthfulness in a story. He often challenged the honesty of his classmates' narrations. On one occasion he questioned a classmate's story by noting, "Mr. Jones [Chad's bus driver] knows where your house is. I can go with him and check to see if your house has a broken window." On other occasions, he challenged the accuracy of the story's details. Chad often clarified ("Dump trucks are yellow, not white") or corrected information when he felt it was incorrect ("No, you have to go *fast* to get a ticket").

Just as truthful details were important for storytelling within the children's classroom community, story length was another important criterion. Chad often encouraged a storyteller to continue with a story if he thought it worthy and honest. When Carrie Elizabeth told about breaking her arm, Chad listened to her opening, and then said, "Tell a lot." He encouraged Danny to tell more about getting a splinter in his foot by saying, "Is that all yo' gonna tell?" Finally, he often suggested that certain children "tell a long story."

Another expectation of Chad's classroom community related to using sharing time as a time to tell a story, rather than a time to force classmates into meeting the storyteller's demands. Chad questioned the storyteller's use of a story if some of the classmates were excluded from a social event. When Angel shared about her birthday (which everyone had heard about for a month), Chad allowed her to say, "I'm gonna have . . ." and then he took over, "I know . . . a birthday party. My mama told me all about it. Some of us got invited!" Other children joined in his game by chanting the events and prizes Angel had offered as incentives. By taking over the sharing, Chad stopped Angel's attempt to share that some children had been invited to her party but others had been excluded.

In this research study (Branscombe, 1991; Branscombe & Taylor, 2000), Charity's rules were different. Because she was an African American child who attended the predominately lower-socio-economic Caucasian school, she attempted to make stories by evoking the stories she had heard from the school books that had been read to her. When her mother was interviewed about Charity's early experiences with literacy, she explained that, because of her husband's and her own work schedules, they did not have the time to read to Charity each day. She relied on Charity's cousins to read their school book stories to Charity every afternoon when they came from school. Those early experiences created an interest in school book stories as well as stories about friends and home.

Charity realized that she could capture the attention of her classmates by retelling their favorite parts of storybook stories during sharing time rather than telling her own story. As a result of this, she did not attempt to tell stories from her experiences but rather commented on others' stories and attempted to conceal details of her own experiences by using published stories. "Bambi makes a good story. Bambi has so many friends in the forest, and he play with them. One day I might get me a brother. I don't have no friends where I just moved."

Even though Charity's notions about her family's and community's expectations of stories differed from Chad's, they mirrored the local African American cultural expectations for their children in that school. Rather than telling the stories of her life, her family and community wanted her to retell the stories of another culture. By retelling the stories of her classmates and their culture, her family and community reasoned that she would not have to justify her culture's social events, behaviors, or values. They hypothesized that if she could successfully retell the other culture's stories, she would be included in the classroom community rather than excluded. Freire's research (1989) reported a similar view of the role of cultural expectations when he discussed cultural invasion in which the controlling group negates a person's view of life. The negation causes that person to experience a sense of cultural inauthenticity and, eventually, to conform to the controlling group's expectations.

Four Literary Constructions Developed during Social Interaction within the Community

After several months of daily sharing and writing in Shared Journal, many children begin to incorporate others' expectations and organization of narratives (i.e. those found in literature, in school, and from peers) with their own. In order for them to make such a transformation, they distance themselves enough from the event so they can shape it into a narrative. They develop a common vocabulary (e.g. language of literature and prose) that they can use to talk about their narratives. They also consider what roles and actions they will allow the people, other than themselves, to take in their narrative. Finally, they make a decision about what cultural rules and norms can and cannot be broken. For example, they resolve questions about whether the storytellers are lying about an event or just fictionalizing it. They decide whether a mistake in their writing (e.g. spelling, punctuation) is a lie that calls for them to be punished or an error that can be erased. In this phase, children experiment with numerous strategies.

Branscombe and Taylor (2000) identified four constructions children use as they develop their narrative voice: if–then constructions, reflections, perspective taking through improvisations, and the language of literature and prose. These are essential strategies for children to develop their narrative voice and move from recounting events to creating narratives. These strategies are theories or hypotheses that the children use to help them distance or decenter from the events they want to share. The strategies free them from the here-and-now and allow them to explore other personas. As a result of the repeated testing of these strategies, until the children discard them because of their limitations, the children move from recounting an event or several events that are somewhat parochial to making narratives with literary qualities that appeal to anyone who hears or reads them.

If–Then Constructions

The researchers found that one of the children's earliest strategies was the use of if–then reasoning. They compared and contrasted their expectations of a story with others' if–then constructions. Because the if–then construction relates to temporal constructions as well as comparison/contrast, such a construction offers children a way to distance themselves from the culture. It also allows them to compare their cultural expectations with other, more distant, perspectives. Finally, it serves as a way for them to begin thinking about sequencing the events of the narrative (e.g. if x happened first, then y would happen next). For example, when Scrap shared about the English preservice teacher's return to England, he said that "If Kate left early in the morning before day and she had to fly six hours to get to England, then it would be dark when she got home."

Reflection

The second strategy for narratives is children's use of reflection as a distancing strategy for making stories from a variety of perspectives. Their daily experiences with making narratives seemingly allow them to reflect on various aspects of those stories so that they become clearer to the narrator. The experiences allow the children the space and support to resolve their issues with story details, lying, mistakes, and the audience. They also let the children safely enter others' roles or lives via their stories. Because of this, none of the children worry that they may lose their reality or their identity because they cannot get out of those exploratory realities. For example, when Scrap wanted to write his version of *Where the Wild Things Are* (Sendak, 1998), he asked the teacher, "Will I be able to go back to my room if I write about the Wild Things' Island?"

During the story-writing phase of Shared Journal, the discussion about their writing and the revision of their stories allow children to move from the public self or persona, who knows the difference between truth and lies, to the narrator who uses a narrative voice that incorporates make-believe to construct stories for an audience. Chad embodies this when he seemingly takes his rules for story and others' stories and coordinates those to create a narrative about stepping on a piece of knife.

Chad Stepped on a Piece of Knife
By Chad

When I was outside an airplane flew over our house just as I stepped on something. It happened yesterday afternoon. My foot was bleeding a little bit. Then, when I got in the house it was bleeding a lot. My foot hurt, but I didn't cry. I'm a big boy!

Blood was on the floor . . . all over the floor. It had purple in it. It had red too! It bled so much that it made my foot die!

My mom was at work when it happened, and my dad, Chris, was cutting the grass.

I didn't step on a nail. I think I stepped on a piece of wood. No, it was a broken piece of knife. It stuck right up into my foot. I had to go to the hospital because of that cut.

Postscript:

You see, it didn't really happen that way. I didn't go to the hospital. I really stepped on something yesterday when I was out in the yard. It's a boo boo, and I wanted to tell a story about it.

Chad demonstrates his knowledge of literature and culture within this story. He builds the story by using stylistic devices such as metaphor, exaggeration, paradox and hyperbole (e.g. his foot bled so much it died). Having the piece of wood turn into a knife also shows his ability to build suspense, use timing, and attend to his audience's interest.

Chad's postscript is the most interesting device. When he actually told the story to his classmates, he sat down, reflected on the impact his story had for a few moments, and then went back to the speaker's chair. The other children asked what he was doing. He replied, "You see. It didn't really happen that way ..." By doing that, Chad showed that he knew that his story violated cultural expectations for a story. He also demonstrated that he was using a narrator's voice, which was more than a recounting of an event, but rather his attempt to construct a narrative that was more like the literature he had heard when his teacher read to the class. He showed his ability to distance himself from his story and then monitor that distance. He also used reflection by attempting to reflect on its impact on his audience. Finally, he invited his audience of classmates to join him as they reconsidered the narrative as if it were from a storybook. Through his narrative voice, he moved from the if–then construction to the as–if construction, which seemingly is a major step in the children's construction of their stories.

Chad was not the only child who attempted to use reflection to develop his narrative voice. Jamie also used reflection to move her scripts into stories beyond her family's, classmates', and community's expectations.

On more than one occasion, Jamie mused about playing "storybook stories." As she discussed her perspective of narratives, she hypothesized that aspects such as accuracy, truthfulness, make-believe, source, and length are essential. She implied that those were the aspects that shaped her story scripts within her dramatic play at Center Time. When Jamie discussed playing *The Tornado Story* at Center Time, she reflected on the tornadoes that her community had experienced before she said anything. She recalled that several children had shared about the damage the tornadoes had done to their homes. She also talked about the ways that she and her classmates played their imaginary versions of *The Tornado Story* in the dramatic play center. Finally, because of the multiple reflections on the details of the tornado stories from her classmates, the journal entries about the tornado damage, and the rehearsal of the imaginary tornado story in the social dramatic play center, Jamie was able to say that she wanted to make a book of *The Tornado Story*. She noted, "It would be as good as Snow White."

Perspective Taking Through Improvisation

Improvisation is the ability to enhance, strengthen, build from, modify, and enrich an existing piece. When individuals improvise, they take the original text and open it to variations. As children distance self from the story, they move into and assume roles within the text. The variations are related to a myriad of elements such as the rhythm, theme, mood, tone, setting, and voice. The variations can be displayed through forms of imitation as well as originality. The improvisation can be a farcical take-off on some other piece. Its satire incorporates imitation with originality and language play with form (Branscombe & Taylor, 2000).

Jamie used improvisation in her written and oral stories in Shared Journal. When she told "The Accident," she embellished a true event in her life. Her embellishment made the story much richer. Although it adhered to some cultural expectations (e.g. cleaning her room), she focused on entertaining her audience rather than cultural accuracy.

The Accident

I got a cut finger. I cut it on the vacuum cleaner when I was cleaning it out. The thing you push down to open the cleaner is where I cut it. My mother lets me clean it out cause it has so many candy wrappers in it. You see, me and my brother, Ron, eats lots of candy and hides the wrappers. We leave the wrappers on the floor in my room. We eat so many candy bars, I have a candy wrapper rug. When my mom sees my rug, she makes us clean up.

This time when I tried to use the vacuum cleaner it bit me. It was mad cause of having to eat all them wrappers. My finger bled, bled, bled and bled till it got through bleeding. It hurt but I didn't cry. My mom didn't even put a band-aid on it. She said, "That's what happens when you eat candy." After it finished bleeding, I went back to work.

Jamie used exaggeration, embellishment of the truth, and humor in this narrative. She knew the elements that her culture expected of a story (accuracy, culturally acceptable behavior, story length) but used them as she chose. Her improvisation occurred as she took a fact and played with it. For example, she stated that her mom let her use the vacuum cleaner to clean her room. She also coordinated the truth, eating candy and leaving the wrappers in her room, with her awareness of the story making. This awareness allowed Jamie to experience the making of shared knowledge (Sinclair, 1991).

Use of the Language and Literary Devices of Literature and Prosody

As children experiment with the writing step in Shared Journal, they puzzle over how they will use their oral storytelling techniques to write stories. Even though Shared Journal requires that children orally share their stories and then write and illustrate them, many children focus on one art form (e.g. oral sharing, illustration or writing) at a time.

Those who love to share their experiences orally quickly realize that their oral story-telling voices, which they labored to construct, will not work for them as writers for readers. This socio-cognitive conflict causes them to contend with their thoughts about the conventions of spelling, punctuation, writing, as well as plot and figurative language. It also causes them to realize that they may have to revise their writings to address conventions so that they can please their audience. At this point, many children realize two things: (1) they need an oral and conventionally written vocabulary for their stories; and (2) they need a style and story structure that is appealing and credible. First, they develop a need for a vocabulary to use as they discuss their stories. This vocabulary includes literary terms, school vocabulary, and real talk. It involves the children discussing ways to spell words and draw letters for those words. For example, the following dialogue occurred between two kindergarten children as they wrote in their journals.

Kelsey	How do you draw a R?
Kyler	See a R. You get a straight line and then you go across. And then you do another one. Right? But, now put S.
Kelsey	Is this your journal?
Kyler	Okay.
Kelsey	How you write S?
Kyler	See how a snake crawls like [child makes wave with arm] and go around. Remember, you spelling Tina.
Kelsey	Oh yeah! T, you go like that. No? How do you make a T?
Kyler	[Shows Kelsey how to make the T.]
Kelsey	How do you write a I?
Kyler	Circle. Straight line. I put a little dot on top. You put a i. You put a A.
Kelsey	Did I do it?
Kyler	N. You know how to make a N, don't you?
Kelsey	No.
Kyler	Look at your date and copy the n.

In addition to conversations about spelling, the children also talk about reading their stories, the genres of the stories, as well as the stories' contents. The following conversation between three children describes what they understand about the importance of directionality in reading.

Amy	I know what my journal says.
Keisha	What does it say?
Candy	Yeah! What does yours say?
Amy	[Begins to read in the middle of her story] Ro____
Keisha	No, you can't switch it over there. You have to do the beginning first.
Candy	Why do you have to read the beginning first?
Keisha	Cause you got to read from the beginning. That's what you do when you read.

Another example details the children's conversation about what is necessary for writing or a written story. The conversation took place as two children looked at their classmate's journal entry that they identified as scribble scrabble.

Tye	Scribble scrabble is writing. It's not drawing.
Zoe	Not either one. Not any of 'em! Cuz that [pointing to the third child's journal entry] don't form nothing. No! It don't form nothing! [Pauses] It seems like … drawing and writing seems like something … Like if you draw something [draws a house with her finger[like a house it's forming something.
Emily	[Points to the scribble scrabble] That'll go in our journals. I ain't put scribble scrabble in my journal.
Tye	When did you stop scribble scrabbling? [The children glare at her but don't answer. Finally Emily answers.]
Emily	Scribble scrabble is like practice writing. I just know how to write now.
Juanita	Yeah! If you scribble scrabble, the teacher'll think you can't do nothing. She'll put them dots on your page and make a big fuss. She'll make you drawed and write letters.
Zoe	Yeah! But if I get mad, I scribble scrabble! I scribble scrabble all over my page! [All of the children giggle.]
Tye	My sister is three years old and she doesn't even know how to write yet. She goes to play school. She scribble scrabbles, but I still like her.

After they begin attending to the vocabulary of their stories, they become aware of how other authors use styles and story structures to keep their readers' interest. This awareness leads them to view reading as more than a grade on a test for reading comprehension. It causes them to study authors' style and story structures. They reason that, if the stories which the authors' write are pleasing to other children, then those authors might have strategies for narratives that they could use. Once this resolution occurs, the children begin studying published authors to give their own stories more audience appeal. Some attempt to make their Shared Journal entries look just like an author's page in a book. Others believe that, if they can illustrate their Shared Journal page in the way the authors illustrated a story, then they will please readers. Some think that conventional spelling is the answer to a wider readership. Others reason that, if they use detail like authors, then their readers would continue to read their stories. These comparisons to published authors allow the children to move to the purposeful uses of conventions such as figurative language, exaggeration, generalizing the past, genre, specific detail, surprise endings, fantasy, and fiction.

Figurative language seems to be a favorite device for many children. They view it as a way to match their words with their story's actions and events, as well as to get reactions from their readers. They also note that figurative language requires less writing than some of the other devices. For example, Annie used figurative language to write about Patrick's brother's accident at nursery school. "Patrick's brother went to nursery school and got his finger smashed. It was flatter than paper and he got a cast." Annie picked a visual image, the analogy of the smashed finger and paper, for her journal entry. She knew the image of a smashed finger that was "flatter than paper" would please and amuse her audience as much as the details of the accident.

Derek's beautifully detailed drawings were trademarks of his earlier journal entries. They often exemplified his interest in visual images. One entry demonstrates this. "Christina's mom dipped some strawberries into white milk chocolate." He created a visual portrait of an action sequence with his word choice.

Clarissa also used vivid detail in her later journal entries. Just like Derek, she constructed her entries from images that related to the five senses. For example, in her journal entry, her imagery related to touch and sight. "We went to see the chickens and two were wet." Then the next week she continued to explore the use of imagery when she wrote, "Brie brought a crayfish and it was greenish brown." Although her entries lack the complexity of combining specific details with action and are one-event narratives, they do cause the reader to visualize two wet chickens and the greenish-brown crayfish.

As children become more sophisticated in their use of narrative voice, they often want their characters to talk through writing or to use dialogue. This interest can be seen when the children begin using bubble captions and dialogue. For example, in one bubble caption Derek wrote, "Favion's mama bought him a sword." In another, he wrote, "Are you sure you want that?" In a third, he wrote, "I'm sure." His choice of short sentences and simple words allowed his readers who had not used dialogue to read and understand that his bubble captions were his way of representing Favion's conversation with his mother.

Some children develop their narrative voices and storytelling ability to the point that they purposefully use fiction and fantasy with their journal entries. They are able to manipulate the actual events to make them more appealing to an audience. For example, Christina fictionalized Anthony's story about helping his father when she wrote, "Anthony got his coat on fire. He was sitting down helping his father put something together." When the teacher asked Christina about her version of Anthony's story, she responded, "I just made it up. It sounds kinda nice. More kids will like it." Even though she added to the actual story, she anchored it in her classmate's reality with regards to what they heard Anthony share.

One of the most complex examples of a child taking a sharing and making it into fiction or fantasy occurred when a child in a first grade classroom wrote a fictional narrative about the chicken pox outbreak in their classroom. The child changed the main character to a chicken. She entitled it "Chicken had the Chicken Pocks." The following text of the story appears as the child wrote it.

Chicken Had the Chicken Pocks

They was a Chicken. He had the Chicken Pocks. The Chicken didn't know he had the Chicken Pocks. He looked in the Mirrow he Cleaned his face. Thene he said, do I have the Chicken Pocks? They was a little bump on his face Thene. He saw some more bumps Yes, I do got the Chicken Pocks He said I'm Itching he said Oh, Oh. That bump hurst I'm Itching I'm Itching All over. The Chicken finally shaved His face but they was still Little bumps. Thene Finally one day

He finally got rid of them. And he gave Theme to his -Mother.-Fater.-Sister.-Brother-The end.

The author of this narrative understands how to sequence events, build on a story structure, use dialogue, exaggerate details, create humor, and use the well-known literary device, anthropomorphism, when she gives the chicken human characteristics (like Lewis Carroll when he attributes human characteristics to the rabbit in *Alice in Wonderland* and Aesop when he has his animals talk in his fables).

Summary

Piaget (1962) and Vygotsky (1978) postulated that children construct knowledge from within rather than being shaped externally. They also point out that children must develop an awareness of their need to become involved in constructing knowledge. This awareness (Piaget, 1976) or discovery (Britton, 1982) allows children to distance themselves from their play or work so that they can build from and use their new, more elaborate understanding. In early literacy development, this awareness relates to children's ability to represent meaning symbolically on the page, so that it includes certain timeless literary qualities (e.g. plot lines, characters, themes, and even forms that are similar to those found in classical literature). Researchers (Bishop & Edmundson, 1987; Branscombe & Taylor, 2000; McCabe & Bliss, 2003; Pellegrini, Galda, Bartini, & Charak, 1988; Silvern, Taylor, Williams, Surbeck, & Kelley, 1986; Snow, Porche, Tabors, & Harris, 2007) have found that both oral and written narrative discourse is essential for success in early literacy.

If children fail in their early attempts to construct a narrative voice, then they become phony and indifferent in their writings or lost in "word swamps" (Elbow, 1998). Those failures often occur because the children lack a classroom process or practice that allows them the opportunity to experience and control their own drawing, writing, hearing, speaking, and reading about their lives and the lives of their classmates on a daily basis. They also need to experience their classmates' perspectives of and reactions to the same experiences and processes that they have.

six
Learning in the Content Areas

Through their participation in Shared Journal, children are continuously talking, listening, asking questions, gathering information, thinking, solving problems, learning about others, and learning about their physical and social world. The purpose of this chapter is to identify and document the content and processes children learn in the social studies, mathematics, and science as they participate in Shared Journal.

The Social Studies

Through Shared Journal, children come to better understand themselves, their class-mates, and their community. They develop beginning understandings of complex ideas related to history, geography, government, economics, and human rights. According to the National Council for the Social Studies (1994), 10 thematic strands form the basis of the social studies curriculum:

1. culture
2. time, continuity, and change
3. people, places, and environment
4. individual development and identity
5. individuals, groups, and institutions
6. power, authority, and governance
7. production, distribution, and consumption
8. science, technology, and society
9. global connections
10. civic ideals and practices.

Through Shared Journal, all of these themes are addressed in a variety of ways.

Coming to Know and Understand Self and Others

When children first enter a preschool or kindergarten classroom, their thinking usually is highly egocentric in nature. This does not mean that they do not think of others, but rather they are unable to differentiate self from others. Their thinking is preoperational in nature as they imagine that most anything is possible, and that everyone thinks the same as they do (Wadsworth, 1971). As children grow and mature, their thought gradually becomes more logical and sociocentric in nature. They become better able to understand that others do not always know the same things that they know and others may know many things that they do not know.

According to Selman (1980), children move through four levels in developing perspective taking during negotiations. Each level reflects an increasing ability to understand and consider the perspectives of others. Selman identified shared experience as one type of perspective taking that moves from a position of no concern for the other's point of view to the point where both parties want to understand the other and be understood by the other. Shared Journal provides daily opportunities for children to listen to the perspectives of others, to identify with each other, and to determine how they differ from others. They hear stories about other children's experiences, and this information helps them begin to understand that things they thought were unique to them have also happened to others. For example, one student named Shawn shared about how he cut his finger while he was outside helping his father mow the lawn. He claimed that it bled badly, and he had to have a bandage to stop the bleeding. Many children identified with Shawn's cut finger. They made comments like, "I know that hurt, cuz I cut my finger once," and "My finger bled too."

On the other hand, they also hear about and come to understand events that have happened to their classmates which they themselves have never experienced. Consequently, through these daily discussions, children come to know their classmates in a more meaningful manner and are better able to determine how they are like them and how they differ from them. This kind of daily experience helps children become more socially aware in their thinking about others and helps children come to know each other in ways that generally do not happen in the classroom. Through these authentic social interactions, children develop empathy with others, learn perspective taking, and build meaningful friendships with their classmates. In a very short period of time, children come to genuinely care about each of the members in their classrooms. The following story exemplifies this.

A Third Grade Teacher's Story

Three people signed in on the sharing board this day. Tyler was the last person to share that day. He can sometimes be silly and try to make the other children laugh while he is telling a story, but this day was different. He started by sharing his morning routine of things he did while getting ready for school. Then he said that he went to his neighbor's house to wait for the bus. While he and his friend were outside waiting on the bus, Tyler's dog, Skippy, ran over to wait with them. They both petted Skippy, and then he started back across the street, but a car was coming and it hit him. Both boys watched it happen.

Tyler was absolutely fine while telling his story until he came to the part where Skippy was hit by the car. It was then that he broke down and began to cry in front of the other children. All of us were stunned! Tyler was not one to show emotion. At this point, I stepped in and asked the children what we might do to make Tyler feel better. Some children suggested making get-well cards for Skippy, and others suggested giving Tyler another dog or a big hug. When it was time to vote, the class unanimously voted for Tyler's story.

What was interesting was that when Tyler began to cry, some of the children began to cry and others just sat speechless. The outpouring of love from this story was unbelievable, and the aftermath has been interesting. Skippy survived and had surgery to repair the injuries received. Tyler brought a picture of Skippy for the children to see. They chose to put the picture on the bulletin board in the front of the classroom, and when Skippy recovers from the surgery, he will be visiting the classroom.

Shared Journal allowed Tyler to express the grief he felt for his dog, an emotion that had been building inside of him all morning. Shared Journal also brought out the best in the children. Their compassion was unbelievable. I was concerned that some of the boys would make fun of Tyler for crying, but just the opposite happened. The children continued to check with Tyler each day to see how Skippy was progressing. I learned a valuable lesson from this experience. The children I work with each day are real people who have real emotions, and they have learned to care about each other. Shared Journal provides the forum and the time for children to talk about things they find significant, to build social understandings, and to cope with things that trouble them. Through Shared Journal children learn strategies for problem solving and for making choices, strategies that nurture coping and compromise, and strategies for showing their feelings and their compassion for others.

Building a Sense of Community

A community can be defined as a group of individuals who live and work together for their common good. As they work together, the children build a sense of caring, trust, and support for each other and for the community as a whole. As children come to know one another through the sharing and negotiating processes, they come to understand, appreciate, and respect the many ways that they are alike and different. This authentic talk helps build bonds of connectedness among the children as they deal with the events they find significant, things they can laugh about, ways they disagree on issues, ways they compromise with each other, and ways they learn to coordinate perspectives.

This process allows all children to serve as decision makers in selecting the story to be written each day. Although, as individuals, they decide if they want to share, what they want to share, and when they want to share, as a group they ask questions, consider options, and make decisions about the stories they have heard, and the ones that they want to record in their journals. They learn to take many things into consideration as they make their decisions, such as how many times a person has had a story selected, which of the stories shared that day has the most potential for retelling, as well as the appropriateness of the content of the story.

As listeners, children hear a variety of details about the lives of the other members in their class and, for the most part, they write about the other members in their class rather than themselves. The only time they write about themselves is when their story is selected as the topic for the day. Writing about the experiences of others is significantly different from most journal-writing approaches that have children write about themselves and their own experiences. Listening to and writing about others' experiences seem to have a profound impact on the children's social development in that they begin to understand how their lives and the lives of their classmates are different, and how they are alike. For example, in one classroom, a first grade student wanted to tell about his father's lingering illness and death. The teacher was concerned because another child in her class had recently lost her father in a plane crash, and she was uncertain of the impact this story would have on that child. After discussing the matter with both parents, they all agreed to let the boy share, but the parents would be there in case of any difficulty that might arise. The young boy told the story of his father's death. When he finished telling this story and asked for questions, the child who lost her father in a plane crash raised her hand. She asked, "How do you feel now?" Then, they began to talk about their sadness in losing their fathers, and it seemed to help everyone in the class.

This documents how Shared Journal allows children the time and place to construct the bonds of connectedness that build a sense of community. In one year, children who participate in Shared Journal on a daily basis learn to use talk as a means to build social understandings, to relate to others, and to cope with things that trouble them both in and outside of the classroom. According to Sarason (1974), the psychological sense of community is

> the perception of similarity to others, an acknowledged interdependence with others, a willingness to maintain this interdependence by giving to or doing for others what one expects from them, and the feeling that one is part of a larger dependable and stable structure (p. 157).

The following are quotes from children that document this sense of community.

> "I like to listen to others share, so I can learn about new things."
> "It helps us learn to take turns and to share."
> "There are happy and sad stories. I felt sad when Zeke shared about his grandpa died, and I know how he felt because my grandpa died one time."
> "The person who is sharing may share about something that we don't know about."

Understanding History

History can be defined as the chronological record of past events and experiences in the life of a person or as a branch of knowledge that records past events in the lives of groups of people. Thus, children are engaging in a discussion of history as they tell about the past experiences in their lives and in the lives of others. The Shared Journal entries written on a daily basis become the historical record of the shared events in the lives of the children in a particular classroom community.

Even at four or five years of age, children exhibit some understanding of the past as evinced when they enter the classroom and say, "Guess what happened to me yesterday!" This narrative approach to their personal histories helps them establish early under-standings (Egan, 1982). However, their conception of the past is limited in terms of the range of historical events known and their ability to think about the distant past.

As the children revisit their own and others' journal entries, they begin to construct the classroom's history, as this rereading allows their thought to move backwards in time, based on the experiences that were shared. According to Cooper (1995), children develop a sense of identity as they explore their own past history. Additionally, they come to recognize that each child's account on any given day is unique in some way that adds to their understanding of the event.

For example, in October the children in one classroom wrote about Paige's hair. Five entries follow.

"Paige had a permanent."
"Paige got her hair curled."
"Paige's hair was straight, and now it is curly."
"Paige had a spiral. Her mama fixed it for her."
"Paige got her hair in a permanent. It was curly, and her mama gave it to her."

The child who wrote only that Paige had a permanent gathered additional information as she read others' accounts of the event. She came to understand that a permanent made Paige's straight hair curly, that Paige's mother curled her hair, and that Paige's curls are called spirals.

Teachers promote this reconstruction each day when they ask children to research in the journals to find answers to particular questions they raise. Questions like "How many of us lost a tooth last month?" or "How many times have we written about someone getting a new baby brother or sister since school started this year?" help children move back in time through their journal research.

Through this rereading of past experiences, children learn to use this history to better help them understand the present. For example, when rereading how Tommy cut his finger while playing with a knife, they remember that it is not safe to play with knives. They also begin to note changes over time. For example, they reread about the day they lost their tooth at a time when they now have a new tooth in its place. Additionally, they begin to use time markers like yesterday, last week, and last month when they talk about the different experiences. They enjoy looking backward in the journals to revisit and remember past experiences. These experiences help them develop a beginning interest in history.

Sometimes the content of the story entered in the journals links to a discussion of historical events. America's involvement in different wars exemplifies this kind of discus-sion. In a kindergarten classroom in 1991, the children voted to write about one child's father serving in Saudi Arabia during the Persian Gulf War rather than about their teacher's recent fall from a ladder. After that sharing, the war became of high interest to her class in that some boys built tanks and missiles in the block center, while two girls built a city in Saudi Arabia. One of the journal entries stated, "I want to go over and cook his [Saddam Hussein's] goose." Another child wrote, "I don't want anybody to get killed." Yet another wrote, "I want Jesus to be in Saddam Hussein's heart." This current war interest led to a discussion of other American wars, both on the homeland and in other countries. This gave the teacher an opportunity to provide instruction regarding the reasons for the Revolutionary and Civil Wars and why they were fought in America. Additionally, the children were comforted as they learned about the outcomes of previous wars. Teachers can build on opportunities like this to engage children in the study of historical events.

Using the Methods of the Historian

By building on children's natural curiosity about stories and their classmates' experiences, Shared Journal introduces young children to the methods of the historian (e.g. generate questions and identify problems, gather information, observe the data, analyze the information, and draw conclusions) and allows older children the opportunity to apply those methods. Because the process encourages children to identify any problems that they have with the storyteller's version of his or her story, they spontaneously generate their own questions to gather information to resolve those problems. They know that the information from their questioning will allow them to make informed decisions about their own versions of the classmate's story. Because of this, they are careful to make sure they have enough detail to discuss and retell the story in written form. During the negotiation step of Shared Journal, the children revisit the information they have gathered. They discuss the story in terms of its authenticity, historical significance within the classroom community, and interest level. Then they make inferences based on their discussion. Their next step is to draw conclusions based on their inferences. In this step, they determine what story becomes part of their historical record of their community. After they have arrived at their conclusion through consensus or voting, they begin writing their stories. Because the Shared Journal stories have happened in the past, they are historical records that are biographical sketches of children's lives. When the children begin writing their versions of the storyteller's story, they become biographers, in that they write their versions of a true story. Although very young children would have difficulty understanding their roles as biographers, older children are capable of understanding that, indeed, they *are* biographers. When the teacher introduces a study of biographies, she can use Shared Journal to document that children have been functioning as biographers. She may then lead them on to reading other significant biographies.

Understanding Government

Children construct knowledge about government through the practice of self-government as they participate in Shared Journal. The children, as individuals and as a group, are the decision makers regarding which story is selected for the daily entry. Because of this important role, they begin to think about fairness and rules of conduct and order as they interact with each other during sharing time. They learn the necessity of the rules and the procedures to be followed as they share with the class and ask questions when others share. This kind of participation sets a precedent for their under-standing of the system of government under which they live. Teachers should discuss the process with children so that they begin to understand why the rules they follow are necessary.

Perhaps the most misunderstood component of Shared Journal is the requirement of selecting only one of the shared stories to be recounted in the children's journals on a particular day. Some teachers have great difficulty with this component in that they fear that the children whose stories are not selected will have their feelings hurt. Sometimes children do get upset when their story is not selected. However, when teachers hold to the practice, they soon learn that this is one of the most important components of the process for building a classroom community. Also, they find that the children are more concerned with sharing and having their voices heard than with having their stories selected as the journal entry.

Teachers can alleviate some of the stress of the voting decisions by entering into the negotiation and deliberation with the children to ask questions related to the details of each of the stories. They can remind the children to think about what is fair related to all of the stories shared and can remind children that they are voting for the story they want to write about and not for the person who shared the story. Additionally, teachers can meet with children whose stories were not selected to console them and to help them better select and present an event that might make interesting stories. Teachers can also suggest that the children whose stories were not chosen go to the book-making center and make their story into a book for the class library.

When children learn to vote, they are learning one vital aspect of the democratic government of the country in which they live. They learn that sometimes their vote is the majority vote, and they are happy about the selection. However, sometimes the votes they cast are not the winning votes, and they have to accept and conform to the majority's selection. Thus, they are learning an essential aspect of democracy (DeVries & Zan, 1996).

After participating in the process for a period of time, children begin to base the reasons for their vote on some significant socio-moral issues. For example, children will vote for certain stories because that person rarely shares and has not had a story entered in the journal. On other occasions, they will vote for a less popular child when they think that their story is more interesting. Thus, through this process, the children are learning to think about and act on issues of fairness, consideration of others' points of view, and moral rightness. Through the showing of this mutual respect, children are learning to think about what is just and right for all.

As the year progresses, children begin to consider the literary merits of the experi-ences shared that day. They think about how they can make a good story out of the experience. When this happens, it is not surprising to find that a child votes for a story other than the one he has just shared. The following is what one teacher had to say about her experience with this governmental issue.

A Second Grade Teacher's Story

The most controversial part of Shared Journal is the voting. Some feel that it is too hard on a child when his story is not chosen. These concerns occurred to me also, but I had heard Dr. Taylor's explanations about how children learn what others enjoy hearing and what makes a good story, so I decided to see for myself. There were days when a child did not "win" and became very upset. Instead of intervening immediately, I watched to see what the other children would do. The community spirit that I saw was amazing. Time after time, another child or small group would go to the upset child and comfort her by saying things such as, "It's alright. My story didn't get written about the first time, but then it did. We'll write about your story later." Or, "Your story was really good, but I felt sad for him because I know that hurt." The children bonded in their losses and identified with each other's feelings in ways that I do not believe would have happened otherwise. Through the stories, they related to each other's experiences. I had never known my students so well, nor had I ever seen them know so much about each other. Children just don't realize how much they have in common in a typical classroom.

While the voting component may be difficult, particularly with young children, they do come to understand the value of and need for this kind of decision making in a democracy. They do learn that you do not always get the thing that you voted for and that you have to learn to accept and live with the majority decision.

Understanding Geography

Concepts of geography are constructed primarily through the children's sharing and the discussions that follow that sharing. Early geographic concepts deal with understanding the world in which children live and their place in that world. These concepts relate to where people are located, what makes different places special, how places and people are related, and how people and things move from one place to another.

Children come to know and talk about the different plants and animals that are close to home. Sometimes they bring their pets to school and share about them. Children who live in the country tell stories about the animals on the farm and how they help provide care for those animals. In the spring, children pick flowers on their way to school and talk about them during sharing time. They love to demonstrate what happens when you blow on a mature dandelion.

Children begin to understand that their mail comes from places that are more distant than their immediate neighborhood. Often they will bring in a card or letter they have received in the mail from a distant relative. Children learn about different locations and what makes these places special as they talk about their homes, the places they like to go to play, where certain events take place, and how these locations relate to each other. Sometimes children attempt to draw pictures in their journal to show the relation between the locale of the story and the school or their home.

Most of the children in the classroom use a variety of location markers that they have in common, like the main shopping areas and the streets that link their homes to the neighborhood and school. When new children come into the classroom, they share information about the places where they have lived and how those places are like and different from the place where they are now living. Additionally, children learn to use location terms like left, right, under, and over as they talk about different locations during the sharing and discussion portion of Shared Journal.

Sometimes children bring artifacts they have acquired from their vacation travels to different states or countries to share during journal time, and they tell stories of what they saw while visiting that state or country and how it is different from where the class lives. This provides opportunities for children to learn about customs that differ from those of their state and country. It also provides opportunities for children to think about their own customs and the artifacts they have at home that relate to those customs.

Weather is another geographical concept that affects children's daily lives. They talk about the weather in terms of how it impacts the particular event they are sharing. For example, "Yesterday it rained hard and the sky got dark. I got scared and was running home when I fell down!" Because their neighborhoods are in close proximity, they share most of the same kind of weather conditions. Thus, storms, hail, and lightening are often used as dramatic elements of the story being shared.

Understanding Economics

Like geography, what children learn about economics comes, in part, through the sharing of stories and the discussion around that sharing. Shared Journal discussions often address two of the key economic concepts, scarcity and wants-and-needs (National Council on Economics Education, 2002). The children often have long discussions about a story that involves someone wanting or buying something.

During one sharing time, Tim shared that he and his mother went to Wal-Mart and bought a pair of Spiderman shoelaces for his sneakers. He told the class that he really needed a new pair of sneakers because his had holes in the toes, but he didn't get them because they couldn't afford them. That same day, another boy shared that he and his dad were going to Wal-Mart when the police stopped them and arrested his dad. The boy said that he ate supper at the jail while he waited for his mom to come and get him. Much to the teacher's surprise, the children decided to write about the child's new shoelaces. She asked the children about their decision, and they responded that Tim needed new shoelaces so he could run the bases in baseball and not fall down. They went on to explain that they had been to jail with their relatives so that was no big deal. This discussion of needs and scarcity exemplifies the kinds of reasoning about economic issues that Shared Journal encourages. It helps children learn what they gain and what they give up when they make choices.

Children often share about the goods that they receive when they go shopping with their mothers. Children share stories of new shoes, new hair bows, and new pajamas. Through these sharings, children come to understand how they are like and how they differ from others in their class. They come to understand and appreciate the fact that getting a new pair of shoes is particularly special to one of their classmates because the shoes he had were very worn. They come to better understand and appreciate how they are economically similar or different.

Learning about Fairness, Justice, and Moral Reasoning

As children negotiate the daily topic and vote on the story they want to record, they grow in their abilities to consider others' points of view, to argue, and to reach agreement on certain topics. Through this kind of negotiation, they are able to co-construct higher levels of moral reasoning.

Young children obey rules in obedience to authority (Piaget, 1932). Whether something is right or wrong is based on the seriousness of the consequences of the behavior, not the magnitude of the misdeed. Because they think rules are set in stone, children believe that the adult decides on and carries out the punishment, and if they disobey, they will be punished. This stage, moral realism, usually ends at seven or eight years of age but may last into adulthood, depending on the child and the child's environment.

The next stage, moral relativism, usually begins to appear around seven or eight years of age. However, with children who participate in Shared Journal in preschool and kindergarten, this appears much earlier. Children begin to view rules as reciprocal and changeable agreements set up by people. They begin to consider others' perspectives, others' feelings, and others' views of them. The oral and written stories document this growth in the children's understandings of making good decisions (the moral compass).

Social interaction and participation in experiences that encourage interaction are two keys to helping children learn about moral rightness, fairness, and justice. When children have daily opportunities to listen to and converse with others, they start to change their earlier notions of rightness and wrongness. They also begin to consider issues of fairness. For example, in a community with high unemployment, a teacher told about her children's discussion of right and wrong. She said that the children had decided that stealing was wrong. They knew that many parents would purchase something as a present and return it after the child played with it for a couple of days. They also knew that some parents would steal presents for their children. During one sharing event, Joey shared that he had a new electronic game. He explained that his dad gave it to him for his birthday. When the questioning began, one of the children asked Joey whether his new game came in a box or a trash bag. Joey explained that it came in a trash bag. He went on to tell about the fun he was having with his new game.

During the negotiation, one of the children said that they should not write about Joey's story because his dad had taken someone else's game and given it to him. Needless to say, the class was most upset by this statement. The child explained that they could write about Joey's new game when he gave it back to its rightful owner. At that point, the teacher realized that the child was applying the class rule of not stealing to the shared situation. After a long discussion, the children resolved that it wasn't Joey's fault that his dad had taken the electronic game. They also pointed out that his dad was just trying to show him how much he loved him by stealing the game for him. Through this kind of discussion about authentic moral dilemmas, children learn to reason about right and wrong. They also learn to show empathy to others and experience it from others.

Mathematics

Number knowledge is a part of logico-mathematical knowledge, a kind of knowledge that is not observable but rather is created mentally by each learner. This knowledge is created as the learner thinks about how objects compare and builds relationships of difference and sameness between those objects (Kamii, 2000). Number relationships that children think about include how objects are alike or different in terms of their quantity, size, and weight. According to Kamii (2000), as children progress in their abilities to think about number, they coordinate earlier relationships so that, for example, "children become able to deduce that there are more animals in the world than dogs" (p. 5). Additionally, they are able to reason that three plus three is six. According to Piaget (1952), number consists of two kinds of relationships, hierarchical inclusion and order. These relationships have to be constructed in the minds of the children as they think about and build relationships between objects and time periods.

Counting and Comparing

There are daily opportunities for children to see the necessity for counting and comparing as they participate in Shared Journal. When they first arrive at school, they look to see how many names are on the sharing board or whether it is empty. If there are fewer than three names, then they reason that there is room for one more if they have something they want to share. This kind of counting is the beginning of addition in that they know if one has signed up there is room for two more, ergo $1 + 2 = 3$.

During the sharing period, all of the children help in counting the number of votes cast and the number of voters present. First, they have to ensure that the number of votes cast equals the number of children in attendance that day, in other words determining a one-to-one correspondence between the votes cast and the number of eligible voters present. Once this counting is complete, they count the number of votes that each shared story received and make a comparison between the three to determine which story received the largest number of votes. The children are using the language and vocabulary of arithmetic as they talk about these totals and comparisons. In addition, they are developing beginning understandings of cardinal numbers in that they come to understand that the final number counted equals the total number in the set. Children in the higher elementary grades determine the percentage of the vote each story received and learn to express these percentages using decimal numerations.

The numbers of questions children ask and the numbers of comments they make during the discussion of the stories are sometimes recorded, either by the teacher or by one of the children in the classroom. The recorder uses these records to announce at different times how many more questions can be asked or how many more comments can be made. These recordings offer more possibilities for counting and comparing.

Numeral Recognition

For young children, there are numerous opportunities to develop numeral recognition in Shared Journal. When signing in, children have to recognize the numerals on the sign-in board. Some teachers have children sign in on a calendar requiring that they learn to recognize numerals that represent the appropriate day. When voting for the story for the day, children count and use numerals to record the total votes for each story. When writing the date in their journals, they record numerals for the day and the year. They also often include numerals in their stories as well as for numbering the pages in their journals. All of these allow opportunities for children to construct the conventional representations of number.

Understanding Conventional Organizations of Time

Each day, the children record the selected shared story on the appropriate page in their monthly journal folder. In doing so, they are required to date that page with the name of the month and the number of the day. This process helps them become aware that each journal has a certain number of pages, that the number of the pages in the journal corresponds to the number of days in that month, and that the pages always follow the same weekly sequence. Thus, in a very short period of time, the children are able to use the previous day's journal page to predict the name and number of the entry date for the new page. Through this activity, children come to understand that every week contains seven days, each of which has a different name, and every month has at least four weeks. By recording the date each day, children begin to construct an understanding of the relationships between days, weeks, weekends, and months of the year. They begin to extend this understanding to develop patterns related to the days of the week as well as number patterns. Additionally, as children look back through their journals for particular events they want to revisit, they learn to use names of the days of the week and the months of the year to find the stories they want to read again.

Through the children's establishment of a one-to-one correspondence between the date on each journal page and the entry of a significant experience, children begin to understand how number is used to quantify time as well as objects. Additionally, through researching the questions that the teacher poses, like how long it took before Tommy got a new tooth or how many stories were written about skinned knees in October, the children begin to think about and understand number related to days, weeks, and months.

Science

The science curriculum includes the study of the life sciences, the earth and space sciences, the physical sciences, and science and technology. In the early years, children must have experiences with different plants, animals, materials, and people in order to construct a knowledge of and ability to use a variety of these scientific concepts. Through touching, smelling, observing, listening, and discussing, children come to understand and use the scientific method of inquiry.

Understanding the Life Sciences

Children learn about the life sciences when they investigate and talk about the characteristics of the living things near their homes and school and as they observe and question the life cycles of both the plants and the animals in their environments. Observation through seeing, feeling, smelling, tasting, and hearing is the primary method used in helping young children learn about living things.

Through Shared Journal, children gain information about the life sciences when they talk about different kinds of animals and plants that are a part of their school and neighborhood. Some may bring samples to share. For example, one child told the story of how he and his father caught some butterflies. They put them in a jar so he could bring them to school. He was able to identify and name the kinds of butterflies he had found and to tell the children where they were found. After that sharing, many children noted that they had found butterflies like the ones shared. Thus, this sharing helped create an interest in looking at the flora and fauna in the neighborhood. When children bring living things to school to share, teachers need to provide the materials and utensils necessary for children to make close observations of the plants or animals being shared. To help children develop interest in the natural world, the teacher can provide magnifying tools to help children look closely at the plants or animals being shared. Other kinds of equipment the teacher may provide might include different kinds of cages and aquariums that could house the animals, and pots for the plants.

Children also learn about the life sciences when they hear stories about animals that others find in their neighborhoods. For example, a second grader wrote the following:

> Jimmy found a turtle in his backyard. He dug a hole in the ground and he found some eggs. The turtle was a mama turtle. The turtle stayed there four days. She came from the woods. I used to have a turtle and his name was Franky.

Children also write about their trips to veterinarians with their pets and the different ways the veterinarians care for their pets.

One particular day, a kindergarten classroom had a very exciting life science lesson when one of their classmates found a snake in the boys' bathroom and told about where it was and what it looked like. Needless to say, the children learned a lot about one local snake, and they voted for that story on that day. These examples show how the content of the life sciences can be discussed and observations can be made during journal time. Teachers can build on this sharing to help children learn more about the life sciences through classroom observation.

Understanding the Earth and Space Sciences

In the earth sciences, children learn about the objects in the sky, the weather, and the properties of the nonliving things on the earth. Children's talk about the earth sciences relates mostly to the things they see around them and to specific weather incidents. They share about how thunderstorms scare them, seeing bolts of lightening, and seeing snow, particularly in those areas where it is least expected. These are the aspects of earth science that children directly experience and that are referred to during journal time. For example, the following journal entries from a kindergarten classroom document how children learn about the earth sciences.

"Alex found a Indian rock."
"Alex got a arrowhead."

Teachers can foster these observations by calling attention to how various plants and trees look at different times of the year. When the children show an interest in the properties of rocks, teachers can suggest making a collection of rocks so that they children can compare and contrast their characteristics.

Understanding the Physical Sciences

In the physical sciences, children learn about the properties of the objects and materials around them, the position and motion of objects, and about heat, light, electricity, and magnetism. Physical knowledge is learned primarily through children's actions on objects, and sometimes children will bring things to share and pass around and let the other children act on and observe. These include things like paper airplanes and prisms. For example, in a third grade class, a young boy brought an airplane he had made at home. The children took the plane outside and took turns trying to fly it. After this event, the children wrote in their journals about how to fly the plane. They talked about the way to hold the plane, throw the plane, and determine when the plane flew the farthest. Children learn about the physical sciences as they act on objects and observe how the object reacts. Teachers can foster this kind of learning when they encourage opportunities for the children to act on the objects being shared.

Understanding Science and Technology

In science and technology, children learn to distinguish between natural and human-made objects and to develop their abilities to use technology for scientific exploration. Teachers can incorporate science and technology through the Shared Journal process. For example, when a child brings in a turtle that he found, the children can use various technologies to explore and learn about the turtle. They can use the interactive white-board for research to determine the particular species of turtle, its habitat, and how to feed and care for the turtle. They may use magnifying glasses and digital cameras to more closely observe and document characteristics and actions of the turtle. They may further construct technological designs for a drawing or three-dimensional model of the turtle. Other technology, such as digital microscopes, may be used to further explore, investigate, observe, and record scientific phenomena.

Teachers must take advantage of the experiences and stories children tell in Shared Journal to provide instruction in scientific content. These stories provide authentic opportunities for the use of science-related technology in meaningful ways. These technologies may be incorporated during the Shared Journal process and/or extended into other classroom activities and learning.

Children as Scientists

Just as Shared Journal provides children with an authentic opportunity to apply the methods of an historian, it also allows children to practice certain aspects of scientific inquiry. It builds on their natural inquisitiveness and provides an appropriate place for their incessant "why" and "how" questions. It presents them with the negotiation step that causes them to reflect on, analyze, and evaluate the information they have about the story. Both of these are essential steps in an inquiry-based approach to science. In addition, Shared Journal encourages children to evaluate their own knowledge based on another's knowledge of a given event or series of events. In order to do this, they have to learn to ask questions like "What matters in this story?", "Is it accurate?", "What parts of the story can I use as evidence to support my point that it is the one we should write about?", or "What are the story's strengths and/or weaknesses?" Finally, they write in their journals.

In addition to applying some of the inquiry-based steps for teaching and learning science, the children use the problems posed by the actual information from the stories to study their physical and biological worlds. When a child shares about riding on the fastest roller coaster at the county fair, some of the children puzzle over the physics of gravity and inertia. They question how the storyteller knew it was the fastest. When a child shares about baking a cake with her grandmother and having the cake fall, some children ask if it got hurt when it fell while others ask what she did to make it fall. Still others, who have baked with their parents or grandparents, ask about the temperature of the oven. When a child shares about visiting the neighbor's chicken yard and gathering a green egg, some of the children question the factual nature of a green egg while others ask whether the egg was still warm when he picked it from the nest.

When children begin writing the stories in their journals, the actual production of the print and picture is a by-product of their scientific knowledge. The use of crayons and markers to represent their stories causes them to consider how they can change or mix colors. The quality of their paper for their pages and how it reacts to colors and pencil marks cause them to realize the attributes of paper. In addition, they have to decide whether they want to offer realistic representations in their illustrations. For example, do they want to color a child's dog purple when the child said it was brown and white?

Summary

Shared Journal provides daily opportunities for children to grow and develop not only in the area of the communicative arts but in the social studies, mathematics, science, and technology content areas as well. The children learn and utilize all aspects of the scientific, mathematical, and social studies content that is introduced through the Shared Journal process. Additionally, they are learning this content through meaningful and relevant social interactions with peers.

part two

The Teacher as Facilitator

Part Two analyzes the implementation of Shared Journal in multiple settings. This implementation is presented through the stories of researchers and reflective practitioners who have used Shared Journal with their students for many years. While some of the teachers have formally researched their use of Shared Journal, others have used reflection and questioning to study children's reactions to the process.

Chapter 7, "A Study of Cases," explores the outcomes of using Shared Journal with children of varying experiences, cultural and developmental levels, and needs. The chapter provides readers with the opportunity to study these variations in four contexts. First, it examines different representations in a kindergarten classroom on a given day. Then, examples from one day's Shared Journal entries in a second-grade classroom are given. Next, it offers readers the opportunity to study a kindergarten student's development in Shared Journal throughout a year. Finally, it provides a fascinating glimpse of adult twins' reflections of their participation in Shared Journal during their kindergarten year.

Chapters 8 and 11 recount two stories from a classroom teacher who uses Shared Journal to meet standards and mandates as well as to assess and document the learning of her students. In Chapter 8, "Meeting Standards and Mandates," the teacher explains how she manages Shared Journal within a standards-based curriculum. She offers options for scheduling, sharing, and negotiation. She also shows how she integrates Shared Journal within her mandated curriculum. In Chapter 11, "Assessment and Documentation," the teacher explains how she documents students' progress and assesses their learning. She also offers options for grading and assessing various areas of the curriculum. Samples of assessments, schedules, and scoring rubrics that could be used with Shared Journal are also provided.

Chapter 9, "Technology and Shared Journal," showcases a classroom teacher who explains how to extend the range of instructional activities with Shared Journal through the use of an interactive whiteboard. She also explains how stories can be recorded and read to peers, family members, and teachers at later dates. She describes how to connect a classroom with classrooms in other communities. In addition, the teacher offers important tips for effective use of technology in the classroom, which include obtaining permissions from parents or guardians, assessing students' understandings, as well as the use of microphones, digital cameras, software scanners, voice-recorder software, and web-based applications.

Chapter 10, "Shared Journal with Special Groups," examines several ways Shared Journal has proven to be effective and successful with special groups of students. It describes specific modifications teachers have used during Shared Journal to accommodate the needs of different children. One section of the chapter is devoted to explaining how to use Shared Journal with children with Down's syndrome, high functioning autism spectrum disorder, cri du chat syndrome, and learning disabilities. Another section is devoted to using Shared Journal with English language learners. A third section summarizes research studies done with pull-out intervention classes that use Shared Journal. The final section is devoted to explaining how Shared Journal has been used in preschool settings.

Chapter 12, "Teachers as Advocates," explains how to promote the use of Shared Journal in classrooms. It points out that Shared Journal is based on research and meets mandates, standards, and children's needs. It offers suggestions for helping oneself and others understand the value of Shared Journal. It also offers help with issues such as students' emotions, students' sharing, meeting standards, making time in the daily classroom schedule, creating a classroom community for Shared Journal, and dealing with change. The chapter provides guidelines for advocating with family members, administrators, policy makers, and community members. Finally, it offers suggestions for administrators who want to implement Shared Journal in their schools.

seven
A Study of Cases

The knowledge, experiences, and developmental levels of students in a given classroom vary tremendously. Teachers are aware of this and understand that they must meet the needs of each individual student. However, many feel unprepared or unsure of how to actually accomplish this in a regular classroom setting, and they report this as one of their greatest challenges (Baumann, Hoffman, Duffy-Hester, & Ro, 2000; Jordan & Stanovich, 2004; Tomlinson, 2004). With the push to meet the continuous improvement targets required by the No Child Left Behind (2002) legislation, many teachers are implementing instructional practices that are not consistent with what research shows is best practice. McTighe and Brown (2005) explain that these practices being implemented include:

1. "broad or overloaded written curricula" that do not address deep understandings
2. "educators' perceptions that they must cover every mandated standard" in preparation for high-stakes testing
3. whole class teaching that models and prepares students for testing formats
4. adoption of a "teaching to the test" method to raise test scores (p. 235).

Ironically, these practices are not resulting in higher test scores. Research examining international educational assessments shows that United States students continue to lag behind many of their counterparts in other parts of the world (Steigler & Hiebert, 1999). The application of common sense also reveals that a "one size fits all" curriculum will not work when classrooms are filled with diverse learners who possess different learning styles, developmental levels, and experiences. It stands to reason that if teachers will work to address students' individual needs and help each student progress as far as possible, rather than providing one type of instruction that may or may not be on many students' levels, then test scores will improve. McTighe and Brown (2005) explain that teachers must address individual differences and provide instruction that "addresses rigorous content while honoring differences in learners' prior knowledge, interests, and preferred learning styles" (p. 236). Fortunately, Shared Journal is a curriculum approach that can be implemented with the entire class while still being adaptable to meet each individual child's needs. All children participate in each step of the process, but they do so at their own individual levels. Because Shared Journal is based on children's stories from their own lives, the curriculum is also relevant, meaningful, and engaging to the learners—all characteristics of appropriate practice.

This chapter will provide examples of cases from Shared Journal to show how individual children develop through the process and how their individual needs are met. Individual cases, cases from several children on a given day, as well as the progress of children throughout the year will be shared. Additionally, a set of twins' reflections as adults on their experiences participating in Shared Journal in their kindergarten classroom will be examined.

Examining Different Representations in a Kindergarten Class on One Day

As stated earlier, the levels of abilities and experiences vary widely in any given classroom. While developing academics for these varying ability levels, Shared Journal also promotes the development of socio-emotional relationships and community. The following examples are extracts from three children's journals from a single day in a kindergarten class. These examples show how a teacher can meet the varying levels of ability in a single classroom, and how a child's academic and socio-emotional relationships develop. Additionally, the teacher's responses to and interactions with these three children will be examined.

Tracy, who shared the story selected by the class to be included in the journal in the following examples, was an African American child who was always clothed in matching dress, shoes, socks, and hair bows. In addition, she was the class "drama queen." Students always knew her stories would be full of intrigue and drama. This particular story relayed her "harrowing" experience with getting sick over the weekend, going to the hospital, and getting a shot. She told with great detail of the shiny metal table she had to lie upon and the shot she received. With Tracy's dramatic storytelling technique, it was not surprising that her story was chosen to be included in the journal. The fact that most children hate getting shots also contributed to the "importance" of her story from her peers' perspectives. Below are three journal entries about Tracy's story representing distinct developmental levels in this one kindergarten class. These entries are from early in the school year.

Martin's representation was one of the lowest developmentally in the class. He has included some closed shapes as well as lines. When he "read" his entry to the teacher, he simply said, "Here it is." There was little attempt to retell or explain the story being represented. After questioning from the teacher, he added that this was about Tracy. For Martin, these marks were representational, but they did not take on any recognizable image. Martin had also not yet differentiated between drawing and writing. This is evident since he did not include any other marks representing the writing for his story. In addition, Martin was not yet able to record the date from the calendar, so the teacher wrote the date on his entry for him. The teacher's questioning (for example, "Tell me about your journal entry. What were we writing about today?") provided the prompt that Martin needed to explain his marks.

Dan's representation is more advanced than Martin's. Dan was able to record the date from the calendar, though he omitted the year. He also has clearly differentiated between drawing and writing. Dan included a pictorial representation as well as "squiggles" that represented his verbalization about the story. When Dan read to the teacher, he said, "I'm sorry about Tracy getting a shot." Dan's story indicates a sense of empathy for Tracy as well as recall of the story. These written squiggles are clearly different than his drawing, and they are beginning to resemble "letter-like" forms. It is important to note the difference in the two types of writing Dan used in this entry. When he wrote the date, his writing is more conventional because he was simply copying the information from the calendar. When he wrote his "story," he was writing based on what made sense

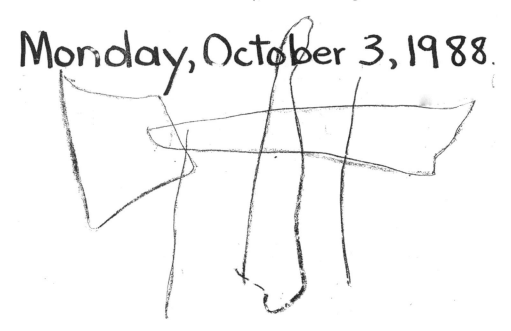

FIGURE 7.1 Martin's Representation on October 3 of Tracy's Story

(I'm sorry about Tracy getting a shut.)

FIGURE 7.2 Dan's Representation on October 3 of Tracy's Story

to him or how he thought the writing should look. This clearly shows that simply copying writing does not indicate a child's true understanding. This is why teachers do not provide written stories or sentences for students to copy.

Dan's illustration provides additional information about the shared story. He includes Tracy lying upon the metal table with wheels as well as the doctor reaching out to examine Tracy. Dan included a body, head, arms and legs, as well as lines representing fingers and facial details. Some of Dan's drawn body parts are dimensional, while others are simply lines. Dan's picture relays additional information he gained from the story telling that he could not include in his writing. The teacher uses this information to help Dan move forward in his representational abilities by building on his strengths and helping him think about his misunderstandings and more advanced representations.

Martine's journal representation is even more advanced than Dan's. Martine has written the full date. Additionally, she included a line under the first line of the date. Often children will begin to draw their own lines showing the teacher that they are ready to begin using lined paper. Martine also shows understanding of the left to right flow of the printed English language, as well as the use of the return sweep as she has written two lines. After the date, Martine has included a sentence about her story. The sentence reads, "i [I] A [am] Sr [sorry] u [you] y [went] t [to] D [the] HSPD [hospital]." With this writing, it is important to note that Martine is using many of the hypotheses children develop as they are learning to record spoken language (Vernon & Ferreiro, 1999). First, she is using at least one letter to represent each word. Typically, that is the first sound or letter in the word. For some words (sorry, hospital), she uses one letter to represent each syllable in the word. In both instances, the letters are phonetically correct representations of the first sound in each syllable. Another hypothesis that Martine is

FIGURE 7.3 Martine's Representation on October 3 of Tracy's Story

using is the letter-name hypothesis. Often children will use the letter that has the same, or similar, name as the word. This can be seen in the use of "u" for "you," "y" for "went," and "D" for "the." The use of "u" is obvious as the name of the letter is the same as the word. Using "y" for 'went' is logical for the child because, as she attempts to isolate the beginning sound for /w/, it makes her think of the letter name for "y." The same is true for the use of "D" for "the." Martine's writing also shows a sense of empathy for her classmate as she expressed sorrow in her writing and included a teddy bear for comfort in her drawing. This is the beginning of building community in this classroom.

When examining Martine's illustration, it is important to note that her mother is an artist. Martine had many experiences of drawing prior to coming to kindergarten. Martine's illustration shows a more advanced level of visual representation. She has drawn her picture from a particular visual perspective. She is aware that objects look different when viewed from a particular angle. Her drawing is looking straight on the objects. She has drawn Tracy lying on the metal table with wheels. Only two legs and wheels are visible because that is all that can be seen from this angle. Additionally, she has drawn Tracy's face looking toward the observer with her arms and feet up and arranged at an angle so that they can all be seen. Her figures are also all dimensional rather than lines as in Dan's drawing. Martine also added a teddy bear to help comfort Tracy. It, too, has its head turned looking at the observer and its four legs arranged in order to be seen. Martine added details including facial parts, skin color, and the beautiful braids Tracy always wears.

These three children are representative of the range of developmental levels within one kindergarten class early in the school year. The teacher must be able to meet the needs of each of these students at the same time. By incorporating simple differences, such as writing the date for those lower level students or interacting with specific questions to guide students' thinking, Shared Journal provides the unique opportunity for teachers to meet individual needs within one curricular approach. There is no preparation of individualized lessons or materials. All of these children participated in the same procedures but at their own individual levels.

Examining Different Representations in a Second Grade Class on One Day

The following cases highlight three children's journals from a single day in a second grade class. These examples show how children's academic development and socio-emotional relationships are promoted through Shared Journal in a second grade classroom. Additionally, analysis and explanation about the entries show how children use varying perspectives for their journal representations. Understanding how to analyze children's journal entries helps teachers better structure their questions and interactions with children to facilitate learning. The story selected to be included in the second grade class journal on this day was about Meagan's sister losing her ring in the swimming pool. The three journal entries provide different perspectives and representations of the story.

Kaley's story reads: "I am sorry that it happened. Did she get it out of the swimming pool? It was a pretty ring. I feel sorry for her. She was Megan's sister. And she felt bad. Megan loved her. She was sad." The illustration shows the blue water from the pool with the ring. Kaley's writing shows her understanding of the use of the period at the end of sentences. She is also using conventional spelling. Her developmental spellings are approaching convention ("swiming" for "swimming," "happn" for "happened"). She incorporates a question, though she does not use a question mark. Kaley also shows empathy for the subject of the story ("I feel sorry for her."), and she expresses how her classmate felt. Kaley's written representation expresses her understanding of the story as well as her feelings about the event.

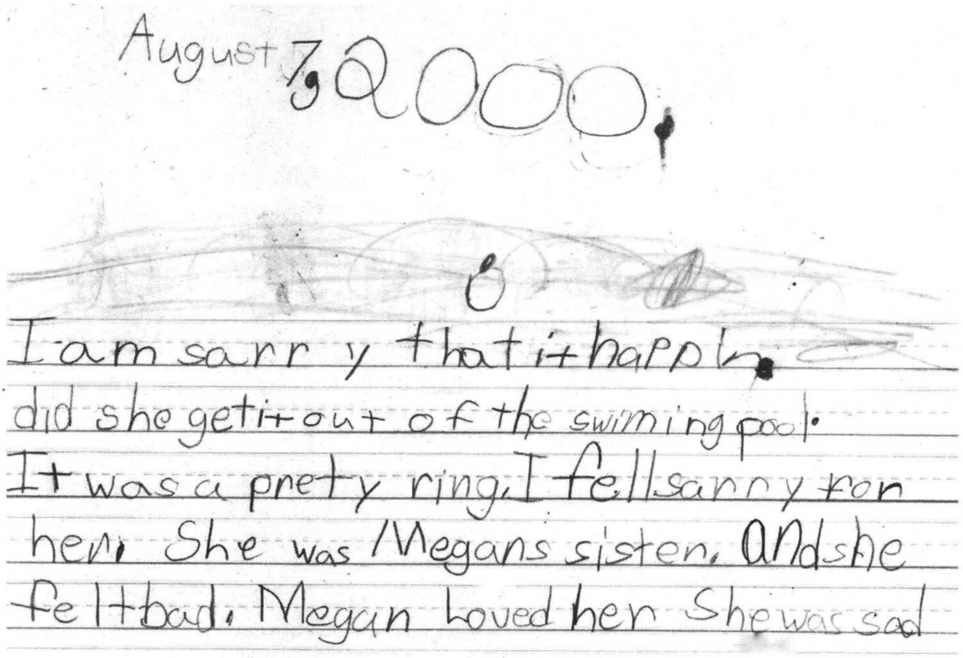

FIGURE 7.4 Kaley's Representation of the Lost Ring Story

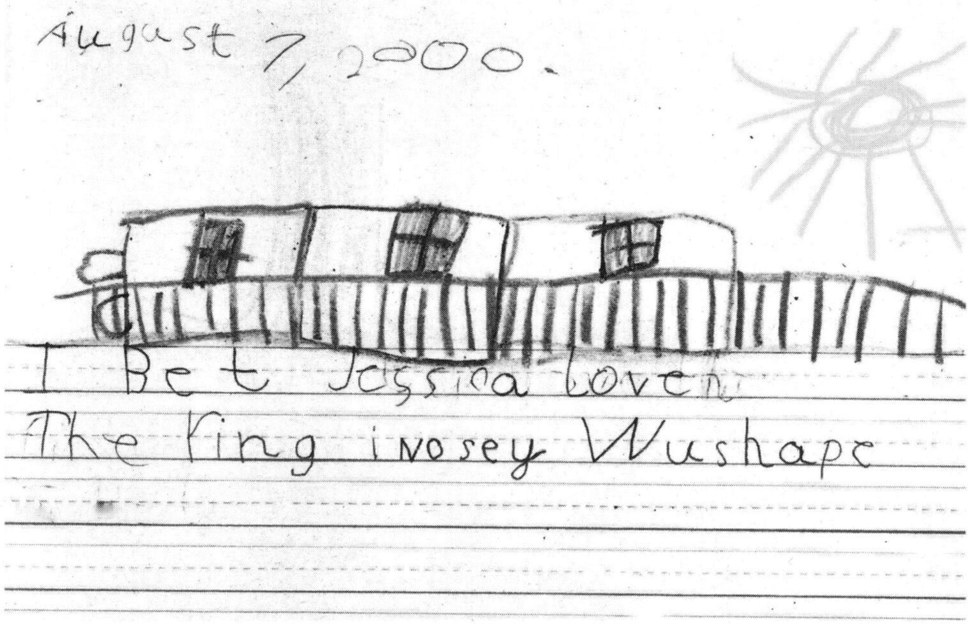

FIGURE 7.5 Meagan's Representation of the Lost Ring Story

Meagan's story reads, "I bet Jessica love the ring. I know [No] she [sey] was [Wus] happy [hape]." Meagan has drawn the trailers behind the fence in the trailer park where she lives. She also included the sun in the upper right corner. Obviously, Meagan's story and illustration provide additional details that she did not include in the telling of her story to the class. Meagan implied in her journal entry that the lost ring was found and that her sister was happy. Meagan's writing includes several conventionally spelled words ("I," "The," "love," "ring"). It also shows that Meagan understands that some words begin with uppercase letters, though she has not yet differentiated the exceptions to that rule. She is also using words or parts of words that she knows how to write. For example, she used "No" for "know." She also correctly represented all of the phonemes as she pronounced them when she wrote "Wus" for "was" and "hape" for "happy."

Hannah took a different approach to her representation of the Lost Ring story. Hannah related the shared story to an experience from her own life and chose to write about that. Hannah's writing reads:

> I lost 6 ring and they [thea] were [wr] like Megan's ring and they [thea] were [wr] my favorite [Fafret] rings and they [thea] were [wr] in [en] a can and I know how [howll] you sister [Sestr] feels [fells].

Hannah has made a relationship between an experience that was shared by a classmate and an experience from her own life. This often happens in Shared Journal, and it is perfectly acceptable and appropriate that she wrote her entry from this perspective. She is still relaying information about the selected story, and she is relating it to her own

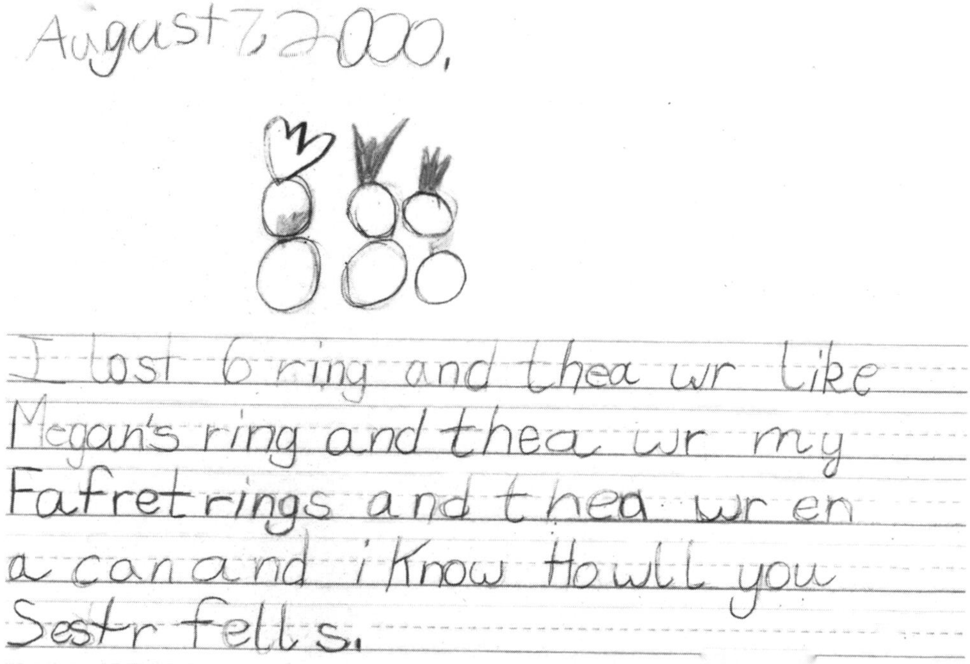

FIGURE 7.6 Hannah's Representation of the Lost Ring Story

experience. This kind of relationship helps build an awareness of the similarities and differences in each other's lives. This is one of the reasons that Shared Journal is such a powerful approach. As explained earlier, Shared Journal develops academic abilities as well as socio-emotional relationships and community.

Examining a Kindergarten Student's Development in Shared Journal over a Year

Daily Shared Journal entries provide an ideal resource for documenting students' development over time. The following journal entries are an example of how one child's abilities progress over her year in kindergarten. The first entry (Figure 7.7) is from early in the school year, October 16, and represents Chrisi's beginning development as she entered kindergarten. On this particular day, Chrisi shared about having an accident. Her story was selected to be included in the journal.

FIGURE 7.7 Chrisi's Entry in October

Chrisi accurately recorded the date from looking at the calendar, although she is having some problems with letter and number directionality. Her entry reads, "I wrote about having my little accident." At this point, she is using one letter to represent each word. Each letter represents or closely represents the initial sound in each word. Chrisi is also using the letter name hypothesis when she uses the letter "X" to represent what she hears initially in the word "accident." Because it sounds similar to the letter's name, she uses it to represent the word. She understands that there are upper-case and lower-case letters, but she has not yet differentiated when she should use them. Chrisi's illustration is of herself after the accident. She drew herself with tears and a sad face indicating that the accident hurt. She is using dimensional drawings for most of her body parts (except the legs), and she included facial details and hands.

In November, Chrisi progressed in her abilities to more accurately represent the sounds in words. On November 5 (see Figure 7.8), the children chose to write about a

FIGURE 7.8 Chrisi's Entry in November

class activity. While learning about frogs in an integrated thematic curriculum study of water, the children learned that one of the longest frog jumps on record was eight feet. They decided to see if they could jump as far as the frog. Each child's jump was measured by recording the number of feet they jumped on the wall in the hallway outside the classroom. Chrisi's entry for the day reads, "I like jumping like a frog. I jumped 4 feet." Her illustration (completed in green to go along with the green frogs) shows her standing beside the number 4 indicating how far she jumped. Chrisi's writing includes the addition of several beginning and ending consonants for some words. She represents "like" by writing "LK" twice (once with a lower-case initial consonant and again with an upper-case initial consonant). She also uses "FG" to represent "frog," "JT" to represent "jumped," and "FT" to represent "feet." Chrisi also is beginning to become aware of punctuation as she uses a period at the end of each sentence in her story.

In January, Chrisi begins to include a baseline by drawing the grass and an upper boundary by coloring the blue sky. She also includes the sun at the top of her page. On January 6, the class got a new student, Christina, so the students decided to write about her in their journals (see Figure 7.9). This was an important way for them to welcome her into the class.

Chrisi's entry reads, "I wrote about Christina. She is new here." Her illustration is of Christina and includes facial details, hands, and feet. She closely represented the clothes Christina was wearing and included her brown hair. In Chrisi's writing, she includes multiple letters for almost every word. She sometimes includes the beginning and ending sounds ("Wt" for "wrote") and other times includes the initial sound for each syllable ("AB" for "about"). She is beginning to accurately represent blends and digraphs ("St" in "Christina" and "SH" in "She"). All of her sound symbol correspondences are accurately represented and continue to show progress.

In February, Chrisi began to space between words (see Figure 7.10). As students read their entries to others and attempt to read their peers' writings, they begin to be aware of a need to space between words. Until they have a need to be able to read their own and others' writings and understand their writing as their speech written down, they see no need to include the spaces. After all, we do not stop or "leave a space" after every spoken word. In this entry, Chrisi also is beginning to use medial sounds (consonants and vowels). Her entry reads, "I like Laura's dress. It is cute." She has progressed to spelling "like" as "Lik" and "dress" as "Jas." She continues to use the letter name hypothesis when she uses "Qt" to represent "cute." As she attempts to sound out "cute," it sounds like the name for the letter "Q."

In April, Chrisi finally stops beginning her writing with "I like ..." or "I wrote ..." Here she begins by telling the reader what her illustration represents. Her entry reads, "This is the Soviet Union flag. We made this flag." (see Figure 7.11). The class was doing an integrated thematic curriculum study of the former Soviet Union. The teacher had taken a trip there the previous summer and the students were interested in learning about her travels. This particular day, the students selected to write about the flag they sewed to represent the Soviet Union's flag.

Chrisi's illustration shows her with a tree and the flag on a flagpole. Her writing includes spacing between the words, and she begins her second sentence on a separate line. She includes several conventionally spelled words ("The," "Flag," "We"). She uses multiple vowel representations, many of which are accurate. She is consistently spelling the same word the same way ("Ths" for "this" two times and "Flag" two times). She is

FIGURE 7.9 Chrisi's Entry on January 6

also using words that she knows how to spell to figure out unknown words. For example, when she wrote "Soviet Union," she wrote "Sov" for "Soviet" and "YouYn" for "Union." She knows that "you" is spelled "Y-O-U," so she uses this spelling in "Union."

In May, Chrisi's twin sister, Carrie, shared about their dance recital. Chrisi's illustration of the story shows great detail (see Figure 7.12). She includes three ballerinas on a

FIGURE 7.10 Chrisi's Entry on February 15

stage with the curtains at the top. Her dimensional figures all have their arms curved over their heads, and each has on toe shoes, complete with ribbon ties. Chrisi's writing reads, "This is a ballerina. We went to go to the ballerina concert." With the exception of one "R," all of the letters and numbers are written in the correct direction. She continues to space between each word and to include several conventionally spelled

FIGURE 7.11 Chrisi's Entry on April 22

words ("a," "we," "to," "go," "the"). For all of the other words, she accurately represents the sounds in the words, including several medial sounds (consonants and vowels).

From the beginning of the year, when she was using one letter to represent each word, to the end of the year, when she uses multiple letters to accurately represent the sounds in words and includes many conventionally spelled words, Chrisi's journal entries show

FIGURE 7.12 Chrisi's Entry on May 9

consistent progress over time. These entries provide a strong example of how Shared Journal can be used to document progress over time. Focusing on students' strengths and their current understandings, teachers can provide feedback and modeling to help each child advance at his or her own pace.

A Glimpse into the Possibilities with Negotiation

On a warm day in early April, a kindergarten class was negotiating with Shauntel about signing up to share her story. Shauntel was a very outgoing student who always wanted to share her stories. She shared about anything she could think of … a trip to Walmart, a tiny (almost invisible) scratch from playing on the playground, a "new" dress (which wasn't really new as the other students pointed out that she had worn it to school multiple times). For Shauntel, sharing was about seeking attention. Each day, she rushed into the classroom in an attempt to be there first to sign up to share. This particular day, however, proved to be a challenge for her. Another student in the class who rarely ever shared had a particularly meaningful story that he wanted to share. The other students found out about his story, and they, too, felt it should be shared. The problem was that there was no empty spot for him to sign up. Shauntel had taken the last open sharing spot, and the students were convinced that her story was not as "important" as their other classmate's.

The negotiation began. The friends gathered around Shauntel and explained their reasons for needing her to remove her name from the sharing board. They appealed to her sense of fairness by taking her to the sharing chart and counting how many times she had shared and comparing that to the few times their friend had shared. They appealed to her sense of moral obligation by explaining how very important his story was and pointing out that her stories were often about mundane, everyday experiences. In spite of all of the appeals, Shauntel stood her ground. It was interesting that no child ever suggested that they or the teacher should just remove Shauntel's name. They understood that this had to be negotiated and that she had to volunteer to remove her own name. The friends didn't give up. They continued pleading, arguing, and explaining their points. Every once in a while, they would stop, move over a few steps from Shauntel to conference about a new strategy, and then they would return to continue pleading with her. Finally, after about 30 minutes, she relented. She rose, went to the sharing board, erased her name, and wrote her friend's name in the now empty space. She turned to the class and announced, "I changed my mind. I think he SHOULD share!" That five- and six-year-olds sat for 30 minutes negotiating for what they believed in is remarkable. The sense of community felt by all of the class members, the respect for each other's ideas even when there was disagreement, and the civilized way they went about resolving this conflict should serve as an example for even the most grown-up of groups. These students had been participating in Shared Journal since they began school in August. They learned how to share their ideas, how to support their positions, how to question others, how to persuade others, and to care for others. All of this development took place during Shared Journal. One can only imagine where these students will go and what they will accomplish having had these opportunities at such a young age.

Reflections from Adults about Participation in Shared Journal during Kindergarten

Teachers often comment about a desire to make a difference in the lives of their students. They often think about their former students and wonder what those students remember from the time in their classes. In July 2009, a rare opportunity occurred to talk with former students, twins Chrisi Jaxon Prescott and Carrie Jaxon, about their memories.

Chrisi and Carrie participated in Shared Journal during their kindergarten year (1987–1988), and over 20 years later they went through their journals and discussed their memories and feelings. This case allows teachers an opportunity to see how one teacher was able to learn how Shared Journal made a difference in her students' lives. It also provides the teacher with an opportunity to reflect on the strategies used and how those may have an impact, not only on the academic learning of students, but also on the social and emotional development, interactions among the children, and lasting relationships that are established as a result of Shared Journal. Finally, it provides teachers with a look at how Shared Journal shapes memory.

The twins and their former teacher began looking through their journals. When asked if they remembered writing in the journals, Carrie said, "I remember writing every day. It was important to us." Chrisi expressed, "It's so funny. It's like you don't know if you remember it or if it's because someone told me. But when I look at my journal entries, I remember about the things that happened." "You forget what it is like through the eyes of a child," Carrie stated. "You don't remember until you see [the journal]. It helps you remember everything you did."

As the twins looked through their journals, they recalled specific events and experiences from their time in kindergarten. Many of the entries helped them recall specific class activities. When looking at the beginning of the journal, they commented on their entries about the gingerbread man. They remembered reading the story, making their own gingerbread men, and then finding out the cookies had "run away" when they opened the ovens. Carrie said, "I wrote 'I wish it would stay in the oven.' Is that the gingerbread man?" Chrisi said, "Oh, I remember that. We went through the school looking for the gingerbread men we made." That activity was used at the beginning of the year to help the students learn their way around the school. As they went from place to place, they found notes telling them where to go next. Their Shared Journal entries helped them recall this event. Shared Journal provides the unique opportunity to provoke memories, both during the year when children are writing, and years later. When looking at an entry about making a replica of a hammerhead shark during a study of water, they both responded, "I remember that." Later, Carrie said, "This was the cave. We loved getting in the cave because we could read in there. We learned so much about bears then." They also found entries detailing a play about various nursery rhymes they developed and performed for their families. "We loved that play. We still remember it. Chrisi was the star for Twinkle Twinkle, and I was Mother Hubbard. I remember it well. It was very important to us," said Carrie. They continued laughing and expressing how fun those days had been.

The review of the journal entries also allowed them the opportunity to remember stories about their own personal experiences. Carrie said, "Mom, remember my accident falling off the jungle gym at Nanny and PaPa's. I drew it. See, it says, 'I fell off the swing.'" Carrie also said, "Aw, our dog, Sam, is in here. Look Chrisi." Chrisi found an entry about a time when Carrie got new shoes. Later they found entries about their ballet recital. Chrisi said, "Look at all your details. The straps on the toe shoes. Everything. Look, I think those are the lights on the stage. You drew so much."

The twins went through their journal entries together, often comparing their entries on particular days. They observed differences in how each of them recorded their representations every day. Chrisi explained, "Carrie, you should see your pictures compared to my pictures. Yours are so detailed, and mine are like circles. Carrie, you were more concerned with your drawing. I wrote more than drawing." Carrie asked, "Did I spell 'watch' right? I did. You did too!" Chrisi responded, "That's impressive. Go us!" Chrisi observed later in the journal that she was "writing two sentences and using vowels," and Carrie said, "I had a reason for everything I included, and it had to be right."

As they looked through their journals and began to notice the changes in their writing, they asked, "Why would we switch to including the letters like that?" They began to get interested in how they developed through the year. Carrie said, "I wrote 'I like mama and daddy coming to school.' But I spelled 'coming' C-M-G." Chrisi noticed, "Now we started writing the date ourselves." She also noticed, "It's interesting that I wrote 'wrote' rather than 'write'. Some entries are present tense, and some are past tense." Carrie said, "I was very detailed in my drawing, and look at these long strings of letters."

During the holidays in December, the children took their journals home and were encouraged to write in them about the events in their lives. Chrisi and Carrie wrote in their journals each day. Carrie read, "I don't like the fire on our table." She asked her mother what that was about. Her mother explained, "That was the Christmas where the advent wreath caught on fire. I looked up and thought there was a fire on the hill across the street and realized it was a reflection from the table. And I came in, picked it up, and threw it in the sink. It was on fire. It was almost up to the light fixtures." The girls immediately said, "I remember that!"

Reading through the journals caused them to recall friends from their class. They asked what others are doing now. For example, when looking at an entry about Amy, Carrie asked about what she was doing now, and her mother said she was now a nurse. They also reminisced about an automobile accident involving one of their former classmates. They were expressing sadness that he still experiences health problems from that accident. Participating in Shared Journal gave them a way to get to know their classmates, to develop relationships, and to form a community. These feelings of friendship and of caring still remain after more than 20 years. Chrisi said, "It's so great that we have these [the journals] to remember our friends and things that happened in school. It is so meaningful now to have these to help us remember."

After looking through the entire journal, Carrie said, "You are more comfortable doing it [writing] as you go. You get more creative and you experiment. It was okay to do that ... to try out new ideas. It [Shared Journal] was really good." Chrisi also observed that she improved in her representational abilities over the year, "Look at the beginning and the end. From that [looking at a beginning entry] to that [looking at an ending entry]. It's so great to have these now." Later, Carrie said, "Your thoughts are more expressive than what you can write [at this age]. You learn to express more what you're thinking through the year. You can express more in the end than in the beginning. You can tell more through my drawings than my writing in the beginning, and I get better at writing through the year. It's great how the journal allowed us to be so creative. We were so different even though we were writing about the same thing." Shared Journal provides the opportunity for all of the children in the class to represent their own ideas about the selected topic on their own levels. It offers teachers an authentic way to develop a sense of community and respect for individual differences. Children's representations are meaningful to them and valued by their peers as they are shared and celebrated.

Overall, it is unclear how much the twins remembered from their kindergarten year. It is clear, however, that going through their journals helped them recall events, feelings, and friends from so many years ago. Through the reflections of these students, it is evident that Shared Journal is powerful and is able to evoke memories, feelings, and understandings in students. Furthermore, it helps teachers see the long-range impact of what they do in a classroom on a daily basis. The students were able to observe the development of their abilities, both in writing and drawing, through the year. Shared Journal provided the vehicle through which these students and their former teacher could reconnect and remember important experiences in their lives. The students expressed strong feelings about how happy they were to have these journals to preserve their experiences. As Chrisi said, "It's so great that we have these [the journals] to remember our friends and the things that happened in school. It is so meaningful now to have these to help us remember." It is also clear that their mother values these journals as she has kept them in pristine condition for over 20 years. Participating in Shared Journal allowed these twins to develop relationships as well as to progress in their academic abilities. Now, more than 20 years later, Shared Journal affords them opportunities to look back and remember their first year in school, their friends, and their experiences.

Summary

Shared Journal is a curriculum approach that can be implemented with an entire class while, at the same time, meeting individual children's needs. The process allows teachers to facilitate all children's participation in each step at their own individual levels. Consistent with appropriate practices, Shared Journal is based on children's stories from their own lives, making the curriculum relevant, meaningful, and engaging to learners. The cases discussed in this chapter highlight how Shared Journal meets individual children's developmental needs and how teachers analyze children's responses and facilitate learning through description of individual cases, cases from several children on a given day, the progress of children throughout the year, and reflections from students looking back at their journals after 20 years. The teacher's careful analysis of and responses to individual children's needs through Shared Journal provide powerful opportunities for teaching and learning.

eight
Meeting Standards and Mandates

A Teacher's Story

Meeting standards and mandates has become the primary focus for most teachers. Administrators, too, continually push teachers to have their students meet higher and higher expectations. Legislators and policy makers tie funding to performance on standardized tests that are, in most instances, aligned with the standards and mandates. While no one argues that there should be accountability, many teachers are beginning to question the teaching methods being used to try and meet these standards and mandates. They ask, "Is it possible to meet standards and mandates while teaching in a manner that is appropriate and engaging for young children?" In this chapter, one teacher, Angela Carr, addresses how she meets standards and mandates through the use of Shared Journal. She explains how Shared Journal addresses the standards within and across multiple content areas, rather than focusing on one content area.

Angela Carr's Story

As a kindergarten teacher, I struggle every year to make time for Shared Journal because I know its benefits. Yet, each year we are given more requirements and are expected to take our students a little bit farther. The curriculum gets pushed down to the point that kindergarten has become the new first grade. Upper grade teachers are very firm and vocal about their expectations of the early childhood teachers. Simply "preparing" students for the next grade is not easy when expectations continue to increase. Students enter our classrooms less prepared, and we are forced to raise the bar even higher. This "pushed down curriculum" is evident even before children begin kindergarten. Just as kindergarten teachers receive pressure from the upper grade teachers, we are guilty of expecting the same thing of the preschool teachers.

The attempt for teachers to be as academically oriented as possible often results in an excessive amount of teacher-directed learning in the classroom. This can hinder students' communication skills. Without the proper balance between teacher direction and child initiation in the classroom, children do not get the opportunities they need to share ideas, play, and solve problems. Communities cannot be developed when children receive direct instruction without student interaction.

As I witness first-hand the disconnection between administrative expectations and developmentally appropriate instruction, I am determined to repair it. Many components of a developmentally appropriate classroom are eliminated when the pressure hits.

These components are often the things that are most critical to child development. These aren't easy to see because they are not tested directly with a pencil and paper test. Successful people are responsible individuals who can express themselves, work well with others, solve problems based on the evidence of the situation, and decide the best course of action considering all who are involved. When do we teach these skills? They are not in the curriculum. They are not mandated by the state. These skills are written between the lines. Yet, if we do not help children develop these skills, we have failed them. Doing what I know is best does make the road a little tougher but a lot more worthwhile. I work to take what I am told to do by my school system and blend this together with what I know children need.

I have learned over the past 17 years that test scores are often used to measure an administrator's effectiveness. These test scores do not take into account how much academic or social progress a school has made. The pressure that administrators feel is communicated to teachers in the following ways:

1. "I expect you to follow the state course of study."
2. "I expect you to use the programs and textbooks that have been adopted by the school system."
3. "I expect your students to perform on grade level or above."

In an attempt to support teachers and ensure quality education for the students, administrators police these expectations. The way in which a teacher teaches the course of study and the manner in which she uses the required textbooks are under constant scrutiny. In addition, it is the teacher's responsibility to communicate to administrators how developmentally appropriate practice not only meets the state requirements but also how it goes above and beyond expectations in developing successful students.

In an effort to communicate how my teaching meets the state requirements, I created a grid to align the components of Shared Journal with our K–3 Language Arts curriculum (see Table 8.1). It is based on Alabama's Course of Study. If your state guidelines differ, you may create your own grid. Take your Language Arts Course of Study and check all of the skills that are taught using Shared Journal. Most of the skills are obvious. However, you will find that, as your children engage in Shared Journal, many more skills are imbedded in this process. These grids are beneficial for communicating with administrators. When they come into your classroom and see you sitting in a circle talking, they need to know what lies under the surface.

Scheduling

Once teachers justify to administrators that Shared Journal is aligned with the curriculum, another worry that they have is how to fit Shared Journal into the day while still following a mandated curriculum. Many teachers have trouble finding time for new methods in an already busy schedule. In my school, I must have 90 minutes of reading instruction in which I only use the required reading program. I also must have 60 minutes of math instruction. This is required by our school system. What I found was that I did not have the block that I needed for Shared Journal. However, I did have the time in 30-minute segments.

TABLE 8.1 Aligning Shared Journal with the Literacy Curriculum

	Kindergarten	First Grade	Second Grade	Third Grade
Sharing the Story	Using words that describe and represent real-life objects and actions	Demonstrating Vocabulary Skills	Selecting appropriate voice tone, gestures, and facial expression to enhance meaning	Demonstrating eye contact, articulation, and appropriate voice intonation with oral narrative presentations
	Listening for meaning in oral communication	Telling a story with a beginning, middle, and end	Using active listening skills	Using figurative language to enhance oral communication
	Looking at the speaker without interrupting	Listening for meaning in conversations and discussions, including looking at the speaker without interrupting	Telling stories and events in logical order	Utilizing precise vocabulary in oral presentations
	Using appropriate grammar and word choice for a specific audience	Using appropriate grammar and word choice for a specific audience	Remaining on topic when speaking	
			Using appropriate grammar and word choice for a specific audience	
Questioning and Negotiation	Responding to stories, asking questions, discussing ideas, and relating events to daily life	Asking questions for clarification	Responding to questions	Formulating questions based on a topic
		Connecting events in a story to specific life experiences	Relating events and ideas to specific life experiences	Evaluating relevant information
	Demonstrating the ability to take turns in a conversation	Generating oral questions to gather information	Answering what if, why and how questions	
		Demonstrating the ability to take turns in a conversation		
Independent Writing	Demonstrating listening comprehension of passages recalling information, characters, setting, main idea, details, beginning, and ending of story	Spelling correctly sight words and single syllable, phonetically regular words	Using correct spelling, including spelling of sight words, spelling of unfamiliar words using phonetic strategies	Composing narrative texts
		Using complete sentences to tell a story	Organizing sentences into a paragraph to address a topic or tell a story	Demonstrating clarity and organization in a composition
	Identifying correct sequence of events after listening to a story	Using narrative modes of writing	Using narrative modes of writing	Using complete sentences, varied sentence structure, and appropriate transition words in a composition
	Demonstrating letter–sound association	Using periods at the end of sentences and capitalization at the beginning of sentences	Using concrete nouns and action verbs in written communication	Using figurative language to enhance written text

Continued overleaf

TABLE 8.1 Continued

	Kindergarten	First Grade	Second Grade	Third Grade
Independent Writing (*continued*)	Printing upper and lowercase letters using proper formation, spacing, and letter-line placement	Using a word that names a person, place, thing, or animal as the subject of a sentence	Describing nouns using adjectives	Applying mechanics in writing, including capitalization of proper nouns and titles of people and appropriate end marks, abbreviations, and commas with dates
	Using correct hand position when holding writing instruments	Using verbs to show action	Substituting nouns with pronouns in writing	Using apostrophes with contractions and possessives
	Stringing letters together to express thought	Using adjectives to describe	Demonstrating correct use of question marks and capitalization in written expression	Demonstrating use of nouns, verbs, pronouns, conjunctions, adjectives, and verb tenses in writing
		Exhibiting proper letter formation, spacing, and letter-line placement in words and sentences	Using commas, abbreviations, apostrophes in contractions, and apostrophes in possessives in writing	Demonstrating use of subject–verb agreement in writing
			Using exclamation points at the end of sentences to show emotion in writing	Demonstrating use of forms of adjectives in writing
			Writing words and sentences legibly with proper spacing in manuscript	Demonstrating the ability to write legibly in cursive
Reading Journal Entry to Others	Publishing through reading or displaying work	Blending phonemes to produce sounds	Reading with fluency	Reading with fluency
	Demonstrating letter–sound association, including matching letters to corresponding spoken sounds and blending sounds into words using printed materials	Blending sounds to produce words	Using punctuation to help phrase	Using punctuation to help phrase
			Reading with expression	Reading with expression
Editing Journal Entry	Using approximate spelling while editing	Editing for spelling, punctuation, and capitalization	Checking spelling with a dictionary	Demonstrating correct spelling in final written text
		Rereading to make revisions	Editing for spelling, punctuation, capitalization, and sentence variety	

A great thing about Shared Journal is that its components can be divided throughout the day. My class shares at the end of each day, and the students negotiate and come to a consensus on the story on which we will be writing. The next morning, the students come in and do their writing. I have found that this process actually helps me add time to the day. The students come in at 7:50, but the bell does not ring until 8:00. With Shared Journal in the morning, students begin writing before school officially starts. They love the structure and the routine of beginning and ending the day in a very predictable way.

I have found that certain students find this routine of special importance. For example, the comfort of this routine is evident with Kelly. Kelly is an autistic student whose mom walks her into class each day. Kelly's mom told me that every morning she looks at the kitchen calendar, tells her the date, and talks about the story she will be writing about in her journal today. If Kelly arrives before I write the date on the board, she does it for me. Then she sits down to write about her friend.

My daily schedule, as shown below in Table 8.2, is an example of how a busy schedule can still accommodate Shared Journal.

Managing Shared Journal Within a Standards-Based Schedule

Every day there are several children who want to share their stories. In my class, I only have time for two students to share each day. This creates a need for a system to determine who will share. A sharing chart, which is managed by the students, helps them do this. The sharing chart is posted beside our calendar. Each time a student shares, he/she colors in a block beside his/her name. When several students come in and want to share on one day, the students go to the sharing chart to see who has shared the most times. For example, if Marcus, Janaya, and Weston all have a story to share and Janaya has shared four times and the boys shared only two times, then they determine that the boys should share. This is not always the case. If a student has a reason why he/she must share that day and the children agree that it is a legitimate reason, they bypass the chart and make an exception. For example, a birthday, broken arm, or baby sister's arrival are all important events that take precedence over the other stories. It takes months for the students to become independent with this.

At the beginning of the year, I am in charge of who shares. When students ask if they can share, I walk them over to the chart and we look at how many blocks are colored in beside their names. Then, it is just simple math. If there are three children who want to share, I ask them to show me who has shared the least number of times. That child is the one who will share. If we have an incident when it is a very special day for a student and he really feels the need to share, I try to guide him with my enthusiasm. I may say, "WOW, your baby sister was born yesterday! I'll bet everyone would like to hear about that. Let's see." Then I ask the students, "Would you like to hear the special news? Maybe Marcus should share about it." They never seem to notice the marks beside the name when it is something special. After a while, the students come to see making allowances for special occasions as the norm.

When I first begin to shift the responsibility for deciding who should share to the students, they are uncomfortable. They want an authority figure to tell them who should share rather than problem solving and taking responsibility for their solutions. An example of this was when three students wanted to share. They quickly figured out that two of the children had the same number of marks by their names. They came to me to

TABLE 8.2 Angela Carr's Daily Schedule

Time	Monday	Tuesday	Wednesday	Thursday	Friday
8:00–8:45	Shared Journal Writing Tier Two	Shared Journal writing Tier Two	Shared Journal Writing Tier Two	Shared Journal Writing Tier Two	Shared Journal Tier Two Computer 8:30–9:00
8:45–9:15	P.E.	P.E.	P.E.	P.E.	P.E. 9:00–9:45
9:15–9:30 Snack	Math Integrated Curriculum Project Work	Art 9:20–10:10 Music 9:30–10:00 Integrated Curriculum Project Work Math	Math	Math	Math
9:30–10:30			Integrated Curriculum Project Work	Integrated Curriculum Project Work	Integrated Curriculum Project Work
10:30–10:40 Bathroom					
10:45–11:10	Lunch	Lunch	Lunch	Lunch	Lunch
11:20–11:40	Recess	Recess	Recess	Recess	Recess
11:45–12:15	Whole Group Reading	Whole Group Reading	Whole Group Reading	Whole Group Reading	Whole Group Reading
12:15–12:35	Reading Group 1 Learning Centers	Reading Group 1 Learning Centers	Reading Group 1 Learning Centers	Reading Group 1 Learning Centers	Reading Group 1 Learning Centers
12:35–12:55	Reading Group 2 Learning Centers	Reading Group 2 Learning Centers	Reading Group 2 Learning Centers	Reading Group 2 Learning Centers	Reading Group 2 Learning Centers
12:55–1:20	Reading Group 3 Learning Centers	Reading Group 3 Learning Centers	Reading Group 3 Learning Centers	Reading Group 3 Learning Centers	Reading Group 3 Learning Centers
1:20–1:30 Clean Up					
1:35–2:00	Rest/Intervention	Rest/Intervention Library 1:45–2:15	Rest/Intervention	Rest/Intervention	Rest/Intervention
2:00–2:30	Shared Journal Sharing/Negotiation	Shared Journal Sharing/Negotiation	Shared Journal Sharing/Negotiation	Shared Journal Sharing/Negotiation	Shared Journal Sharing/Negotiation

ask me what to do, and I asked them to think it through on their own. After several more attempts to get me to make a decision, they gave up and went back to huddle around the sharing chart. Soon two children emerged and signed up to share. I was so proud that they figured out a solution. I approached them and asked how they came to an agreement. They responded with, "Jamison said we could do it." This surprised me so I asked, "Jamison? Why does Jamison get to decide?" They looked at me like I was crazy and said, "Because he's the line leader today." They wanted someone to make the decision for them. Since I refused, they found another leader. I realized that this was a tough decision for them to make on their own.

However, even when deciding who should share is just simple math, it does not always go smoothly. For example, in January when the students were accustomed to handling the chart on their own, there was a huge argument. I looked across the room to see Kelly running around with the marker. Several children were gathered around the sharing chart, and one was chasing her around the room. I called them all over to the chart to have a group discussion. I asked Kelly to count and see how many times she had shared. She said, "Four." Then I asked her how many times Weston had shared. She said, "Two." My next question was, "So who has more marks?" She responded, "Me." I continued with, "Then who should get to share?" Once again she responded, "ME," and she took off running again with the marker.

These examples illustrate that teaching students responsibility and independent thinking cannot be achieved instantly. It takes guidance, patience, and a good sense of humor. This should be thought of as a continuum that requires the teacher to help the students become aware of their roles in each step of Shared Journal. For example, they have to become aware of their roles during class question/answer sessions, voting, and even sharing. As they are gaining an understanding of their roles, the teacher provides them with strategies for being successful with those roles. The teacher may suggest that students ask "how" questions as well as "what" questions. She may suggest that when students cannot hear another student's story or question, they could ask for the student to speak louder. Teachers can also provide strategies for helping students to think about or reflect on their reasoning. The teacher may ask them to use facts as they talk during negotiation. She would model this for them by asking probing, reflective questions ("Was that what she said in the story?" "Did that happen on her trip to the store?" "How did she say they found the turtle?").

The final step in this process is that the teacher has to realize and be ready to relinquish control of the Shared Journal discussion. Her role shifts from managing Shared Journal to monitoring and facilitating the students as they become independent thinkers and learners. As the teacher helps the students become more responsible and independent, she is addressing citizenship standards in the social studies curriculum.

Scheduling Options

The length of time required for Shared Journal can be overwhelming at first. Teachers often ask if Shared Journal can be modified to take less time. My response is that they have to find what works best for them and their students and modify the process accordingly. Some teachers choose to have one child share each day because of scheduling issues. Other teachers have shortened the Shared Journal time by assigning the students a "sharing day."

In reality, these time-saving measures often hinder the authenticity of the sharing experience. Students want to share experiences in a timely manner. For example, if they have to wait a week to share about losing their first tooth, their excitement is lost. Like-wise, if they have to wait three days to share about their dog getting hit by a car, they lose out on the community support of their peers at the time that they need it most. I encourage teachers to follow the steps of the Shared Journal process until they are comfortable with it. Once they understand the process and the purpose of each step, they are better able to make modifications to fit their busy schedules.

Sharing

In my classroom, two stories are shared each day. Every morning, the students sign up for sharing. The students write the titles of their stories instead of their names. I have them do this to shift the focus from the student to the content of the story. When it is time to share, the students share in the order that their stories are written on the board. The class is sitting on the carpet in a circle. This sitting arrangement is beneficial because it promotes conversation and a sense of community among the students since they can see everyone and make eye contact during the discussions. The child who is sharing a story sits in the sharing chair. In my classroom, I use a tall director's style chair so that the student can be easily seen and heard.

When students have finished sharing they ask for questions and comments from the group. The helper of the day records the comments and questions on the board by using tally marks. He/she will announce when five comments and five questions have been recorded. At the beginning of the year, I record the number of questions and comments. This system of recording whether or not a particular student makes a comment or asks a question has many benefits. First, it helps the children learn the difference between a question and a comment. I help them do this by modeling. For example, if someone says, "Did your sister go with you?" I might say, "Great *question*, we do need to know who else was there. I am glad you *asked* that." I do the same thing for the comments. If a student says, "I have been to the beach, too." I might say, "I am glad you let us know that. Your *comment* relates to the story. Good *comment*."

Next, recording questions and comments limits the discussion, making every question critical for gathering information. The students quickly realize this, and they do not want to waste a single question or comment. For example, a student sharing the story tells us that his cat is brown, and another student asks the question, "What color is your cat?" That question is wasted because the audience already knew this information. The group will respond with, "We already knew that" or "Someone just asked that question." The same applies for comments. If the student shares about getting hurt on the playground and someone makes the comment, "I have two puppies," the comment was wasted because it does not relate to the story. I help the children by saying, "Does that comment relate to the story?" The students pick up on this quickly and will often call out, "Doesn't relate" or "That's not what this story is about."

Limiting questions also helps us develop better questions. For example, a favorite question of kindergarten students is, "Did you have fun?" Well, if the student went to a water park and ate ice cream, then we can bet that she had fun. I will interject and say, "Can you tell us what you did that was the most exciting part of your trip?" This helps the students learn to really use their questioning to gather information for their writing.

An additional benefit of recording questions and comments is helping children attend to the importance of number. When recording questions on the board, I model for students how to figure out how many more questions or comments are left. They learn to announce this information during the discussion. This also helps them monitor the difference between questions and comments. For example, they often say, "That was a comment. Comments are all filled up."

Negotiation

When the students are finished sharing and the questions and comments are exhausted, it is time for negotiation. Each aspect of Shared Journal meets various standards and mandates, and the negotiation step is no exception. This step addresses standards related to oral language development, debate and persuasion, telling and retelling stories, logic, reasoning, and considering others' points of view.

To initiate negotiation, I lead and act as a model. First, I ask the students to think about which story they would like to write about in their journals. Then I point to one side of the carpet. "Everyone who wants to write about [*title of story*], move to this side of the carpet. "Everyone who wants to write about [*title of story*], move to the other side of the carpet." The students are separated enough so that there is a clear division between the groups. The children then sit down. I call on individual students to try and persuade the others who are voting on the opposite story to come over to the story that they think is more important. When someone changes her mind and moves to the other side, she must tell the group what made her change her mind. (If children are talking out of turn during the negotiation process, they must go to their seats. This means that their vote will not count.) We continue this until everyone who wants to speak has had a turn, alternating between sides of the carpet. Students become familiar with this process quickly. The helper of the day soon becomes the mediator of negotiation. I am always there for assistance if needed.

After the students have had several opportunities to persuade others, I ask them the name of the story about which the class will be writing. The story with the majority of students is selected. The students can usually tell by looking at the groups; sometimes they have to count. Everyone writes about the same story in their journals. Before the children leave the meeting area, I recap the chosen story by asking, "Who is the story about? What happened? Where did they go?" They then write about this in their journals the next morning.

Curriculum Integration

The curriculum grid discussed above (Table 8.1) aligns the Shared Journal components to the Language Arts Course of Study. However, Shared Journal covers much more than the communicative arts. There are daily opportunities for curriculum integration. Sharing often involves mathematics and geography. For example, the helper of the day records the questions and comments on the board with tally marks. Once there have been five comments made and five questions asked, then question time is over. The helper of the day announces how many more questions and comments are remaining throughout the discussion. When Natalee shared that she had owned her puppy since she was a baby, someone asked, "How long ago was that?" We took time to figure out the answer to this question. When Alan shared about going to Texas, we found Texas on the map and talked about the direction you go, how long it takes, and the states you go through to get there. When students share about a special event, such as their birthday party, we find it on the calendar and count how many days ago it was or how many more days until the event.

The interaction among the students and the discussions that transpire are far greater than the required objectives. I could teach all of the required objectives and skills without Shared Journal by using isolated activities and assigned journal topics. However, Shared Journal makes it real. It connects the standards that are being taught to the real world of the students. If those standards are taught in isolation, we lose valuable student interaction. This interaction leads to better understanding of the world around us.

For example, Jamison shared about his uncle's "Pit Bulls." The interaction that occurred during sharing time provided the students with an opportunity to expand their vocabularies and clarify their understandings of the meaning of "bulls." They learned that some bulls are classified as cattle but some dogs are named bulls because of their appearance. They learned this as Jamison shared about what color his uncle's "Pit Bulls" were, what their names were, and that they lived in his uncle's backyard. During question and comment time, Marcus asked, "Do they have horns?" Marcus thought that Jamison was talking about actual bulls. He had no prior knowledge of pit bull dogs. This gave us the opportunity to discuss what a pit bull dog is, and Jamison described in better detail what they look like. This example also shows that students learn to critique the speaker and question the validity of the story. Jamison has exaggerated the truth on many occasions, especially during sharing time. When the negotiation began, Natalee said, "I don't believe he played Hide and Seek with those dogs." Another child spoke up and said, "Me either. You know dogs can't count." This kind of interaction cannot be measured or checked off on a checklist, yet it is an excellent example of critical literacy in that it allows children to analyze the information from the discussion and to make informed decisions. It also allows them to use the context of the conversation to try to make sense of the story so that all have an agreed-upon understanding. Natalee had some knowledge that pit bulls can be aggressive dogs, and another child focused on the rules of the game of hide and seek. Through their discussion, the students were able to create a new understanding and appreciation of Jamison's sharing.

Summary

Shared Journal is valuable to teachers because of the student objectives that can be measured. Shared Journal is just as valuable to the students for the objectives that are difficult to measure. Students are given an authentic purpose to share, lead, discuss, negotiate, compromise, and come to a consensus. The lessons they learn during sharing time reach far beyond any curriculum guide or course of study.

Through this chapter, I have attempted to document how Shared Journal meets required standards and mandates. I have also shown how I allotted the time for Shared Journal so that it does not interfere with the work I am required to do regarding mandated programs and curriculum. Teachers have the professional responsibility to not only meet standards and mandates but to also provide engaging and authentic instruction for their students. Shared Journal allows me to do just that.

nine
Technology and Shared Journal

As educators, we often hear about the twenty-first century classroom and the importance of implementing technology. We know that, if technology is used as a developmentally appropriate tool in instruction, education can be revolutionized. As with most things, this is much harder than it sounds. Many classrooms around the world have been outfitted with very expensive high-tech products. However, many of those products serve only as dust collectors because educators simply do not know how to implement them for daily use. Technology will never replace teachers, but teachers who do not know how to implement technology will eventually be replaced.

The purpose of this chapter is to discuss ways that one teacher, Sandy Armstrong, uses technology to extend the range of instructional strategies for Shared Journal. This chapter will focus on the use of the interactive whiteboard to document how technology can naturally and easily be integrated throughout the entire Shared Journal process. It will also include how to utilize microphones, digital cameras, email, websites, recorder software, conference software, scanners, different types of memory (computer), video cameras, printers, and voice recorder software. In addition to discussing the actual use of the various kinds of technology, the chapter will discuss how the use of technology helps students develop and increase their literacy abilities, as well as address the other aspects of Shared Journal (history, time, friends, number, story, audience, moral reasoning and community). It will also describe how technology helps teachers and students document growth more efficiently and effectively during Shared Journal. The chapter will discuss how the use of technology allows teachers and children a myriad of opportunities to share their work with others. Examples of the various uses of technology with Shared Journal discussed below can be found on the book's companion website.

With the advent of interactive electronic games and videos, today's popular culture has pushed teachers to utilize interactive technology in their classrooms. This technology must be sophisticated enough to compete with the video games the children use on a daily basis. When teachers use technology with Shared Journal, they are building on the children's interest and topics of conversation by joining their worlds of electronic games and interactive videos (Olson, Kutner, & Beresin, 2007). In addition, technology allows the children to connect with people outside of their classroom, city, and state so that they become members of larger communities.

Use of the Interactive Whiteboard in Shared Journal

Interactive whiteboards have several brand names such as SMART Board, ActivBoard, Memio, and Promethean. The interactive whiteboard allows teachers and students to interact with the content from a computer by way of a whiteboard surface. Anything that can be done on the computer can be projected onto the interactive whiteboard. In addition, information can be manipulated and added with pens and/or fingers. The research into the use of interactive whiteboard is in its infancy; however, early studies (Swan, Schenker, & Kratcoski, 2007) are documenting that the use of whiteboards improves student learning because students actively engage in making representations and building relationships. Additionally, the students have others comment on and/or challenge their representations so that they revisit their original offerings and either revise them or argue for their validity. The whiteboard also makes learning more interactive (Cuthell, 2005; Miller, Glover, & Averis, 2003; Painter, Whiting, & Wolters, 2005).

Whiteboards are replacements for traditional flip charts, overhead projectors, and chalkboards. They not only offer an enlarged visual means for students to see content and material from lessons but also offer an interactive component so that students can interact with that content (e.g. drawing, writing, graphing) on the whiteboard. They are excellent tools for demonstration. For example, if a child writes a letter backwards, the teacher can manipulate the letter to show a mirror image or write the conventional form of the letter and drag it over the child's representation to help the child visually see the differences. Furthermore, the whiteboards can use downloaded research and information, provide virtual field trips, and have students participate in videoconferences. The fact that teachers can record and save instructional moments is a major advantage of using the whiteboard. In Sh,ared Journal, the interactive whiteboard offers teachers an instructional strategy that is easy to use, can serve as a recorder, and engages all of the children, no matter their expertise with technology.

Signing up to Share

Using an interactive whiteboard is a very convenient way for students to sign up to share during Shared Journal. Teachers can set up this step in multiple ways. One option is to have each child's name at the bottom of a whiteboard calendar. Then the child drags his/her name to the date when he/she wants to share. If the teacher saves the calendar each day, it becomes a class record that can be pulled up before sharing time. The children often develop a rule that only those children whose names remain at the bottom of the calendar can sign up to share. Because they can see how often they have shared and see their classmates' names who have not shared at the bottom of the calendar, they start thinking about who needs an opportunity to share. This thinking leads to the students' development of a sense of fairness in dealing with others. Using the whiteboard technology allows flexibility in that children can change who shares on a given day. However, these kinds of decisions need to be monitored by teachers and students to ensure fairness.

Another option for using the whiteboard calendar for signing up to share is to have children actually write their names in the day's space on the calendar. This can be done in several ways. For young children, the teacher can leave the names as models at the bottom and have children copy the spelling of their names. If the teacher has children with special needs, she can use a split screen allowing the child to write on a blank page to limit the distractions and increase focus. The teacher or child then drags the child's writing to the correct calendar block. Also, the teacher or child can touch the names written on the whiteboard and hear those names spoken through the computer as they were recorded by the child, the teacher, or the child's classmates. This works well with English language learner (ELL) students as they not only get to hear their names but also hear the names of classmates. Another option is having the children drag their photographs onto the calendar day when they wish to share. This is helpful with young children who are having difficulty with name recognition. The teacher can also combine these various strategies to meet individual children's needs or begin by using the photographs at the start of the year, increase the difficulty by transitioning to printed names, then to having children write their own names as their abilities progress.

When children are signing up on the calendar, numerous instructional opportunities and teachable moments emerge. For example, when Amber wrote her name on the whiteboard to sign up to share, she inverted the "m" in her name and wrote "w." The teacher noticed the letter inversion (Awber) and decided this would be a good opportunity to help Amber. The teacher drew a lower-case "m" on the whiteboard and then dragged the correct formation of the letter "m" over Amber's "w." As a result of the teacher's strategy, Amber realized that the two letters were not the same. Amber stated:

> When I have a toy car in my hand and make it stand on its head, it's still the same thing. When you turn a letter on its head, sometimes it's magic cause it can turn into a whole new letter.

Through the use of the whiteboard, Amber became aware of the importance of directionality and had a new reason to understand the importance of representing the letter correctly.

The calendar can be saved each day with one click on the interactive whiteboard. When the teacher does this, she can easily keep up with how many times each child has shared for the entire school year. In addition, the teacher can analyze the data and create tables and charts to document growth for individual children or the entire class.

Preparation for Sharing with the Class

Through the use of "The Information Organizer," the interactive whiteboard helps children plan their oral sharing before they share with the entire class. An "Information Organizer" is similar to a story map and includes the journalistic five w's (who, what, when, where, and why). It can be in the form of a table, so that the child puts written notes for each question in a square. It can also be in the form of drawings and drawings with writing. The teacher can assist the child as he fills in each aspect of the story in the appropriate square on the interactive whiteboard. The Information Organizer can then be displayed on the whiteboard as needed. This strategy helps with preparation for sharing as well as questioning and writing.

Sharing with the Class

The interactive whiteboard allows the children to record their oral stories during Shared Journal. The recording tool allows the children the opportunity to hear themselves at a later date. Some teachers immediately replay the stories after the child has shared so that they can add details or make clarifications. Others use the recordings for children who are absent or involved in pull-out programs so they can hear the stories once they return to the classroom. ELL children use the recordings to listen repeatedly to the stories to make sure they understood the child's story. The teacher can also post the oral sharing time to a website so others can hear and note progress in the students' oral storytelling. Teachers can use a microphone and record everything the child says with software that comes with the interactive whiteboard or use a free computer program, such as Audacity (www.audacity.sourceforge.net). These recordings are also great resources to save in the child's digital portfolio.

Questioning for More Information

The recorder and microphone tools within the interactive whiteboard are invaluable in the questioning step of Shared Journal. The microphone helps children understand each other and resolves arguments. For example, a child may ask questions that have already been answered. The other children may point this out and request a replay of the questions so as to show what was in the discussion. The replay makes all the children accountable by having immediate proof of what was shared.

When the Information Organizer is used during questioning, it helps children keep up with the vital information needed to fully understand the story. For example, when a child asks a question that has already been added to the Information Organizer, another child may say, "Look up there. She's already answered that question." The Information Organizer often plays a major role in which story is selected. For example, when Bailey could not answer the children's questions about her story, they voted to write about Hilyah's because she provided them with all of the details.

Writing Titles or Key Words for the Stories

In Shared Journal, students record titles or key words for the topics of their stories to assist in remembering the various stories that are shared. All students love to write on an interactive whiteboard because they get to use different tools for visual effects. For example, on a SMART interactive whiteboard, children can use the "fancy pen" (which allows them to write in multicolored digital ink), clipart, and a spotlight feature. Using it for this step of the process not only encourages hesitant writers to participate in writing but also spotlights the abilities of the artistic child. Using the interactive whiteboard also makes it very easy to change or make modifications to illustrations or texts. For hesitant writers, this can be especially helpful as it relieves fears of making mistakes.

Another way that the teacher and children can use the interactive whiteboard for writing titles or key words utilizes a "Sound Sheet." This sheet is similar to a small document that children may use when referring to the alphabet. It includes the upper- and lower-case letters along with pictures that begin with the initial sounds for the letters. On the whiteboard, children may tap the letters or blends on the "sound sheet" and hear the sounds. This helps them remember the sound and think about how they may use each letter in their spelling.

The interactive whiteboard is large enough for the entire class to view and participate in the writing of the titles or key words. The children can assist in choosing and spelling each word if the writer requests assistance. Another way the interactive whiteboard can be used in this process is to document a student's thought process by using the recorder feature as he writes the title or key words. This feature records the drawing or writing on the whiteboard and allows the teacher to review the child's thought process as he or she was writing.

Negotiating and Voting

The interactive whiteboard recorder or a free audio recording program, such as Audacity, can be used to record the discussion during the negotiation and voting steps of Shared Journal. This allows the teacher and children to record and then listen to children's justifications about the selection of a story for the journal. It also provides the teacher with helpful information regarding how children relate to one another. Hearing the recording of themselves provides opportunities for children to think about others' points of view, the merits and aspects of the stories, and reasons for persuading others during voting. Also, it allows them to revisit their negotiations so they can reflect on their arguments and evaluate their reasons for choosing certain stories as journal entries. Because the interactive whiteboard is so simple to use, the children can revisit their recordings during other times of the day.

During voting, the interactive whiteboard can be used for tallying votes. The automated response system or clicker can be used, allowing the teacher to show the results immediately in a variety of ways. For example, the teacher can use a bar graph or pie chart and have the children interpret the results to determine the story selected for the journal.

Recording the Story in the Journal

Although the children write the stories in their traditional journals, teachers often allow some children (special needs, hesitant writers, or children with behavior issues) to rewrite their stories on the interactive whiteboard. This provides extra motivation for these students. Teachers also use the interactive whiteboard to share the children's stories with people outside of their classrooms. This use of technology allows students to reach beyond the boundaries of their classrooms and share their work in a very real and authentic way.

Another way to encourage writing is to use a scanner to digitally capture the child's picture that he/she drew about the story and then let the child use the recorder on the interactive whiteboard to tell about the picture. This recording can then be replayed and stopped as needed so the child can write what he/she said. This can be particularly helpful for children with special needs or those who have difficulty remembering their stories and focusing on the writing at the same time.

Reading to Peers and the Teacher

Teachers can use a video recorder (in a computer or traditional video recorders) to record the child reading his/her story. These stories can then be shared with others. The recordings can also be added to the child's digital portfolio to compare progress throughout the year.

Celebrating Progress

Using the various types of technology mentioned throughout this chapter makes celebrating children's progress easy. All of these technologies allow for documentation and saving of the various steps in Shared Journal. This documentation from the entire Shared Journal process can be stored and recalled for celebrating progress at various times and in multiple ways. Also, digital cameras may be used to take pictures of the children to be displayed with their work. Children enjoy using digital cameras and love seeing their pictures.

The easiest way to organize the child's saved work is by using digital portfolios. These digital portfolios are exactly like student portfolios that are kept in file folders except they are kept on the computer. On the computer, each child will have a folder with his/her name. Within the student folder, there may be numerous other folders labeled as Shared Journal, Math, etc. As students complete work that needs to be saved, this work is saved in the specific folder on the computer. Teachers should take care to develop the folders at the beginning of the year to provide an easily accessible way to organize and store all of the digital work samples. If this is not done, the amount of files can become overwhelming and prevent optimum use of the information. Children can easily learn for themselves the process for saving documents.

Getting Permissions

In order for children to be able to freely use and participate in all activities that involve technologies, it is important to get written permission from their families. Unlike other activities within the school and classroom, technology is a public forum. With technology, classrooms and the children within those rooms become visible to family, friends, and strangers. Such public exposure requires that teachers ensure that children's privacy and safety are addressed.

Every parent should receive a release form. This form allows parents to give or deny permission for their children to be included in pictures, web pages, videos, university projects, etc. The form explains how this involvement provides many opportunities for teachers and students to share their work samples and projects with others. Teachers or schools should be thorough in developing this permission form so that it includes all circumstances where the students' work or images might be used. This prevents the need to have families sign multiple forms. If families do not give permission, teachers are aware, and precautions are taken to respect the children's privacy.

Connecting Communities

Technology allows for collaboration between schools, as well as within the classroom. For example, teachers and children at Auburn Early Education Center (AEEC) engaged in a literacy mentoring project with high school seniors in Sage Hill School in Newport Coast, California. They participated in this project because teachers wanted the kindergarten children to make connections to the world outside of Alabama. Through the use of Bridgit software, the SMART interactive whiteboard, and SMART recorders, the children shared their Shared Journal stories with the Sage Hill School seniors.

In this literacy mentoring project, the teacher and children engaged in Shared Journal. Once the children had written and illustrated their stories in their journals, they scanned those stories to the computer to be displayed on the interactive whiteboard. Then, the children who chose to share their entries read their stories. The highlighter tool was used as they added the commentary necessary to explain the illustrations for the stories. For example, one child named Malik had a speech problem that caused him to be very shy. He would not talk to anyone but the teacher. Over time, he used the interactive whiteboard with his stories and began to share with his classmates. He wanted to share one of his stories with the Sage Hill seniors. For this entry, Malik's illustration was very detailed and colorful, but his text consisted of only one sentence. Because of this, he used the recorder and highlighter feature to explain his illustration and expand his story. The SMART recorder is used throughout this process. Using Bridgit software, the seniors from Sage Hill watched recorded clips from the students at AEEC. This interchange between the schools culminated in a real-time discussion about particular stories.

Developing a Record of the Stories Included in the Journal

After the children have written their stories in their journals, a child records the title or key word of the story on a monthly calendar on the interactive whiteboard. This is then put on the class website, sent home as a printed hard copy each month, and placed in the bound journal at the end of the year. This helps the children and others recall which stories were included for each day.

Using Technology to Assist with Assessment

As described above, the interactive whiteboard is invaluable in Shared Journal. All student work on an interactive whiteboard can be saved and put in a child's digital portfolio, emailed to families and administrators, used as a form of assessment, and used to provide an account of each child's progress. The information can be saved on a computer, burned onto a CD, saved on a flash drive or a portable hard drive, or put on a website. Sharing this information allows families to become more involved in their children's education. It also helps parents to interact and engage in conversations with their children. Because they have knowledge of what is happening in school, the stories that are shared, and the children's journal entries, families are able to ask specific questions, eliciting better responses from their children. Saved items can also be shared by printing, emailing, or sending via computer memory.

The plotter printer has also been used in Shared Journal. Using this type of printer makes it is very easy to create a print-rich environment in classrooms, in hallways, or other areas. The plotter printer can print work on the interactive whiteboard on all sizes of paper, including poster size.

Using Web-Based Applications with Shared Journal

Another area of technology that can be very effective with older students using Shared Journal is web-based applications. These applications are free, making them very accessible. Some examples of web 2.0 applications are blogs, wikis, social networks, digital storytelling, and video-sharing. Web 3.0 applications are currently being developed and promise to be more precise and even more powerful than the 2.0 applications. The future of technology has no end in sight. Because of this, Shared Journal will continue to be increasingly powerful and effective in conjunction with future technologies.

One of the most exciting areas of technology for use with Shared Journal is having a ubiquitous computing environment (van't Hooft, Swan, Cook, & Lin, 2007) for all of the students and the teacher. With the use of the Internet, the students, on their individual laptops, could visit various sites as a student shared about visiting a grandparent, going to Disney, going shopping, or seeing a play. As a result, the student questions could be less generic and more specific to the story being shared. If a student shared about a specific object, the classmates could download information about that object. Finally, the teacher could help the students develop strategies for coordinating the information from the Internet with the story being shared by the classmate.

Using these web-based applications, such as blogs or social networks, students can share their stories with their families or other classes. Students could develop web-based publications of their stories, blogs of their classroom experiences, or wikis announcing exciting new stories added to their web pages. Using all of these applications comes easily to students growing up in a technologically savvy world and provides a way for teachers to engage students in ways that are meaningful to them.

Summary

Technology can be used to enhance Shared Journal. A variety of technology applications may be incorporated in each step of the process. The use of technology promotes children's deeper understandings and engages them in interactive learning that is meaningful and familiar. Technology is the avenue for moving Shared Journal beyond the walls of the classroom so that others may participate and enjoy the process. Technology allows children to move from the sole use of paper, pencils, and crayons into the digital age.

ten
Shared Journal with Special Groups

Johnny came running down the hall and into the literacy intervention classroom. Out of breath, he asked, "Is it sharing day? Cuz, man, I got a story to tell!" Three months earlier, he sulked into the intervention classroom, never volunteered to speak, hated to write, and had very little confidence in his abilities. This "turn around" is one example of how using Shared Journal with special groups of students can produce amazing results. This chapter will examine several ways Shared Journal has proven to be effective with special groups of students as well as specific ideas for modifying the process to fit the needs of different children.

"The importance of attending to individual learning needs in America's classrooms has reached a critical level as diversity multiplies across the student population" (Brimijoin, 2005, p. 260). Shared Journal is an excellent approach for meeting the individual needs of diverse learners so that they experience success. Very little modification is needed for students to experience such success.

What makes Shared Journal work so well with special needs children? Why does it work with few modifications while other classroom strategies, with modifications tailored to a specific special need, fail? Shared Journal offers children a classroom environment that is accepting and fun. Because all of the children are treated equally, the special needs children can be "regular kids" who feel a sense of attachment and belonging to the classroom community. They have as many opportunities to share, ask questions, write about, and read as their classmates. During the time the teacher and children participate in Shared Journal, the special needs children do not have to worry about the transition process of being pulled away from their classrooms for special services. They can just belong.

Many adults do not realize that special needs children have so many interventions, academic coaching, and support services during the school day that they do not feel a sense of belonging or attachment to a classroom community. Their schedules often preclude the opportunity to interact with peers, make friends, share feelings, or communicate with others. They can feel lonely and fearful of how to interact with their classmates. They may not have the time to experience the social interaction necessary to develop who they are outside of the label adults have given them. When the teacher uses Shared Journal with them, they have opportunities to interact with others in authentic ways. They must listen to others' stories and questions so that they can ask a question that is not laughed at or share a story that is valued. Because of Shared Journal, they have the opportunity to adapt to the other children and build on their strengths and uniqueness.

Shared Journal with Students with Special Needs

Shared Journal has been used successfully with students of many differing abilities. Students with Down's syndrome, high-functioning autism spectrum disorder (ASD), cri du chat syndrome, learning disabilities, and other special needs have participated successfully in Shared Journal with no modifications. (See Chapter 2 for the steps in the process.) For some children, minor modifications may need to be made. Other students may need gentle guidance to stay focused or to complete the writing of their stories. For example, one student with Down's syndrome needed the teacher to help her get started with her writing. She wanted to see what others were writing rather than writing herself. With this guidance in getting started, she was able to successfully represent the story in her journal.

Language development is often one of the most impaired domains of functioning in children with Down's syndrome (Abbeduto, Warren, & Conners, 2007). Children with Down's syndrome are, however, often able to overcome their limited language abilities by using "less sophisticated forms of expression" (Abbeduto et al., 2007, p. 254). Shared Journal allows these students to use stories from their own lives, ones with which they are personally connected and very familiar. Because the content is meaningful to them, they are able to focus more on how to relay their stories to others rather than remembering the content. Teachers have also found it helpful to "rehearse" some children's stories with them prior to sharing. Some make use of an Information Organizer, which helps children think about the who, what, where, and when of their stories. The organizer is basically a chart or table where the child or teacher can write or draw symbols to represent each aspect of the child's story. The child can then use the organizer as he tells his story to provide memory prompts for the sharing. An example of the Information Organizer can be seen on the book's companion website.

A young girl with cri du chat syndrome participated in the Shared Journal method without the teacher having to make any modifications. Kristoffersen (2008) explained that many children with cri du chat syndrome have small receptive and expressive vocabularies, and their articulation may include omissions, distortions, and substitutions. They also tend to have better receptive language than expressive language. While this young girl with cri du chat syndrome did not ask questions, she did share about getting a new dress. The teacher allowed her to participate verbally on her own terms, and she was always able to listen to others' stories and represent those in her journal.

Shared Journal has also been successfully used with a child with cerebral palsy. Her aide drew what the child wanted in her picture, and the child colored the picture. The child told her story to the teacher, and the teacher wrote what the child said on the journal page. The child also was able to tell the teacher about the picture and story while they were interacting about her journal entry. In addition to the special needs children mentioned, children with language disorders due to serious physical problems such as stuttering, hearing deficit, mental retardation, and traumatic brain injury can and do participate successfully in Shared Journal.

While students with ASD display a wide range of abilities and difficulties, research has shown that many young children with autism are delayed in their vocabulary relative to their mental ages (Charman, Drew, Baird, & Baird, 2003). The pragmatic aspect of language development can also prove challenging for these children. Loveland, McEvoy, Tunali, and Kelley (1990) found that autistic children included more awkward verbalizations or inappropriate utterances as they participated in telling or recalling stories.

In a summer enrichment program, one autistic boy started the Shared Journal session by hiding behind a bookshelf. As the days progressed, the teacher sat with him. He listened carefully each day to the sharing of stories and scribbled something in his journal. By the end of five weeks, he had moved himself to the outer circle. During the summer enrichment program, he never shared or joined the circle, but he always listened and wrote about the story in his journal. He was given the opportunity to participate in the manner that was comfortable for him.

Another autistic child had to have his assistant sit by him. If he needed to rock, he did. To help the other students understand his autism, the teacher and his mother held a class meeting to discuss his behaviors and needs. This helped his peers understand his behaviors and, as a result, the students ignored his rocking. He shared, asked questions, and recorded his representation of the story in his journal. Lanter and Watson (2008) recommend literacy intervention strategies for students with ASD, such as encouraging story retelling, reading and writing about students' personal experiences, and using dialogue to construct meaning. All of these are present in Shared Journal, making it an appropriate approach for children with ASD.

Children with Asperger's syndrome, which is included in ASD, also engage successfully in Shared Journal. It can be more challenging for them because of their tendency to be long-winded, persevere on one event or topic, and fail to consider their listeners. In addition, when they share or ask questions, they often speak in a monotone voice and violate personal space, which presents difficulties for their listeners. When the teacher modifies the Shared Journal process with a timer for sharing a story and asking questions, Information Organizers for the story's structure, and a picture book for the steps of the process and transitions during the process, the children are most successful.

A Teacher's Account of Joshua Sharing

Joshua has autism. One day Joshua said that he wanted to share about making gingerbread cookies. He had made them in his other class. In order for him to share this story a script was made for him to read and look at during his sharing time. Included on this script were pictures to help him remember all the details of this cooking activity. We also let him practice before getting up in front of the class. After sharing, the most wonderful thing happened. If only you could have seen his face. He was smiling the most incredible smile that I have ever seen from him. This was the first time I had ever seen him show so much expression. His special needs teacher happened to be in the class during sharing this day, and she had tears in her eyes and so did I. If anyone doubts that sharing does not promote caring, they wouldn't after seeing this story being shared.

As Joshua and his teacher showed us so well, Shared Journal invokes feelings from all participants. As children share stories about their lives, others make connections . . . from relating the story to something that happened in their lives to sharing joys and sorrows to celebrating accomplishments from children like Joshua. All of these feelings help develop community in the classroom. A common bond is built through our stories.

We have implemented Shared Journal successfully with a student with severe developmental delays. She participated in Shared Journal each day in a summer enrichment program. This student was wheelchair bound and unable to communicate except through sounds. She often cried to leave the group during other aspects of the summer program but always wanted to join during Shared Journal. When the teachers tried to get her to leave the room during the sharing, she would wail and cry until they allowed her to return. Although she could hold a pencil, she could not make letters or draw representational illustrations; she scribbled in her journal each day. By the end of the summer enrichment program, she raised her thumb or finger to vote for the story about which she chose to write.

Some students with physical needs may require special modifications or equipment in order to successfully participate in Shared Journal. Most often, these are the same modifications they use in the classroom for other activities. Students with minor hearing difficulties are asked to sit close to the person sharing. This allows them to be able to participate and hear the stories. For students with more severe hearing difficulties who need hearing devices such as hearing aids and cochlear implants, teachers have used special equipment such as microphones and receivers. Whoever is sharing the stories wears the microphone and restates the children's questions so that the hearing impaired child can hear and understand. It has been amazing to see how quickly all students adapt to using these technologies and are willing to assist their peers in participating in Shared Journal.

For students with speech difficulties, sharing can sometimes prove difficult. They share their stories, but the other students may have difficulty understanding. Some teachers have found it helpful to practice with the student who is sharing before sharing time so that she knows the story. The teacher can then help with key words as the student shares; care should be given to only provide key words. Because the other students begin to understand each other's strengths and needs, they often ask "yes/no" questions to make it easier for the student with speech difficulties. While the students with special needs are able to share their stories and participate in representing stories in their journals successfully, the other students in these classes are developing greater understandings of, and respect for, people with diversities. This builds a strong sense of community and mutual respect not always found in classrooms of young children.

When children with special needs are participating in a regular classroom setting, some teachers have found it helpful to have a class meeting with the child and his or her parent. The parent starts by telling about the child's condition. The child can add to the discussion. The other children then ask questions; they often ask questions such as, "Will he ever get well?" The teacher, along with the parents, explains what the children can do to help the child. The child with special needs is then allowed to do what he or she feels comfortable doing (e.g. sitting in the circle, sitting on a carpet piece/square, sitting with an assistant, asking a question, or rocking). The teacher makes sure the child with special needs records a representation of the story in the journal each day. The representation is on the child's developmental level (scribbles, drawings, writings).

These minor modifications have enabled children with special needs to participate successfully in Shared Journal in regular classroom settings.

Shared Journal and English Language Learners (ELLs)

Edgar, a kindergartener whose native language is Spanish, began his participation in Shared Journal by drawing pictures. While Edgar spoke very little English, he used his acquired language to "read" his stories and to share. For example, after drawing about a friend's new blue shirt, he said "Blue" to read his story. The teacher used his language and expanded by saying, "I see that you drew your friend's new blue shirt." Bauer and Manyak (2008) explain that language-rich classrooms are "ideal for accelerating ELLs' oral language and academic vocabulary development" (p. 176). Because Edgar was immersed in the English language at school, and he was motivated to communicate with his friends during Shared Journal, Edgar's acquisition of English progressed rapidly. Ernst and Richard (1995) explain, "Children learn their first language by using language as a means to communicate with real people in real situations. The same applies for students learning a second language" (p. 326). Shared Journal provides opportunities for all ELLs to communicate, both verbally and in writing, about real events from their own lives. For children like Edgar, Shared Journal provides a way to participate just like their native English-speaking peers.

When working with non-native English speakers in Shared Journal, some teachers have made extensive use of picture dictionaries to aid in understanding vocabulary and events from shared stories. They have also used Internet resources to create picture cards for commonly occurring themes, characters, and settings in Shared Journal. For example, in kindergarten classes, children often share about losing teeth. Picture cards depicting teeth or children with loose teeth are used as aids in conferencing with students prior to and during writing.

In addition, teachers of students who speak limited or no English often review the main details of the shared story (who, what, when, where, why, etc.) using interactive whiteboards to create simple illustrations for each of these aspects of the story. (See Chapter 9 for examples of the use of interactive whiteboards.)

Another strategy that many teachers use is the Diglot Weave approach. This is a strategy that helps the students move from their familiar language to the language they want to learn. Similar to the rebus methodology, the Diglot Weave has the teacher insert key foreign words into the story. This can be used in Shared Journal when children or the teacher write notes, titles, main ideas, or journal entries. For example, after a child shares about her new dress and records the key words or title of her story as "New Dress," for a Spanish-speaking student the teacher would write the following: "Nuevo Dress." The Diglot Weave inserts key foreign words (in this case, the English word "Dress") while still using some familiar native words (in this case, the Spanish word "Nuevo").

Shared Journal with Pull-Out Intervention Classes

Research has shown that Shared Journal is highly successful when used in intervention classes where children are pulled out of the regular classroom for periods of time to work individually or in small groups with an intervention teacher (Garner, 2008; Gunnels, 1992). Garner (2008) decided to try a modified version of Shared Journal in her literacy intervention program after watching her first graders struggle with mandated writing assessments. The intervention program was for students in first and second grades who were struggling with literacy. The program was designed to provide intensive, daily intervention with the students to increase their literacy abilities. They were then to be phased out of the program when they were performing at grade level. The goal was to provide specific, intensive intervention based on students' individual needs and help them progress to an average level of performance as quickly as possible.

Garner became frustrated and knew that she needed to better meet her students' needs after observing her intervention students in their regular classroom settings as they were given a testing preparation assignment to write on the topic: "If I could go anywhere in the world, where would I go?" The students had blank pieces of paper in front of them. As the teacher watched, she noted that her students stared off into the distance, waiting for an idea to come. Their frustration seemed to build when a few of the other students began writing something on their papers. Little did the intervention students know that their peers were simply copying the topic from the board. It did not matter. The pressure continued to build and, eventually, the students simply shut down. These struggling students were failing. They had negative attitudes about writing. They felt great frustration over what to write. They also had strong feelings of inadequacy.

The intervention teacher knew she had to try something different. After learning about Shared Journal in one of her graduate courses, she thought it might work. Because Shared Journal is based on children sharing stories from their own lives, she thought this approach might be more meaningful for her students. They could share stories from their lives, stories that were important to them. This could provide them with an opportunity to think and write about issues that were very familiar and free them to concentrate on their writing in general rather than on an isolated topic to which they might not be able to relate. The teacher decided to develop a modified process of Shared Journal that would allow her to continue her required intervention methods while, at the same time, find time for Shared Journal.

Modifications to Shared Journal

The Literacy Intervention Program was a daily pull-out program with small groups of students (from three to six students). The students were in a Title I school with 99% qualifying for free or reduced lunch. The students stayed in the intervention classroom for approximately an hour each day. The process of Shared Journal was modified and included three days each week. The remaining two days were spent implementing mandated programs. Other modifications included having only one student share each day. With the very short time frame, there was no time to have multiple students share. Since only one student shared a story each day, the need to negotiate and select a topic was also eliminated, saving additional time. All of the other steps remained the same. The student shared the story, questions were asked for further clarification and information, the topic was recorded on the board, and students represented the stories in their own ways in their journals. The teacher acted as a facilitator throughout the process, interacted with students for one-on-one teaching during their writing, and students shared their writings with each other and the teacher. The teacher also celebrated journal entries when students made attempts to incorporate new conventions or techniques. The teacher occasionally had the students share their entries with their regular classroom teachers to celebrate their progress and to help advocate for the use of Shared Journal with other teachers.

After examining the results of her study, the teacher found improvements in two areas: writing and attitudes. All (100%) of the students showed improvements in their writing. The specific areas of improvement included literary qualities, organizational qualities, language qualities, and writing conventions. The students began to add more details to their stories and organize them in a sequential manner so as to "create a movie for the reader to watch as he or she reads" (Garner, 2008, p. 25). One student, who initially had difficulty establishing meaning, used phrasing and vocabulary to inform the reader. For example, one of the student's initial entries read: "When it was my birthday I went to my Grandmama homes and at the skating rink. After that I came back to my Grandmama homes to jumpin on the jumpin sad day." This early entry showed his inability to match feelings and events. One of his entries at the end of the intervention read:

> Sunday Courtney went to a Easter party. Courtney play at the Easter party. He play with the jumping bag. He won one. He got a surprise because he won. He got a lot of eggs. He found the golden egg. He ate hot dog. He found 15 baskets.

This later entry showed his ability to sequence events and clearly establish meaning for the reader.

The children in the intervention group added punctuation, capital letters, and phonetically spelled words to their writings to make it easier for the reader to follow their thoughts. They also used more detailed pictures to help illustrate the meanings of their writings. In all, they were more proficient in their writing abilities after the introduction of Shared Journal.

Perhaps the biggest change in the students after introducing Shared Journal into the intervention program was in their attitudes towards writing. Initially, the students were hesitant to participate in Shared Journal. The teacher began by modeling and posing questions about the shared story. The students were reluctant to answer. The teacher encouraged them and asked them to think about what makes a good story to share. Their initial responses were, "I don't know," "good ones," or no response at all. By the end of the intervention, the students said that a good story to share was one that included their friends or one that made their friends laugh. They moved from an unwillingness to share their opinions and respond to others' opinions to willingly sharing their stories and responding to the stories of others. They began to ask questions that were purposeful and helped to develop the story. For example, in a story about visiting Chuck E. Cheese, a local pizza restaurant, the students wanted to know who went with them, the games they played, and at what time they returned home. These questions required the student sharing to add information to his story rather than simply retelling what was already shared.

The most exciting change was the improvement of the students' relationships with each other. They developed personal friendships with the students in their pull-out session. They began to appreciate each other's life experiences. The teacher noted one specific day when a student shared about the first time he met his father. The other students were excited for him and were eager to write about his time with his dad at Burger King. The students respected this child's special memories. Shared Journal gave them an opportunity to get to know their group members and develop closer relationships. It provided a safe and secure place for them to share their lives. For these children, children who were struggling, this kind of experience is invaluable.

Another Example of Shared Journal in a Pull-Out Intervention Program

Shared Journal has also been used successfully in other pull-out intervention programs. In this study (Gunnels, 1992), Shared Journal was used in addition to other literacy activities. The intervention program took place over nine weeks and included daily, one-hour sessions. The intent was to provide an intensive, short-term intervention to try to accelerate the participating students' literacy acquisition. The participating students were all identified as the lowest in their first grade classrooms and in danger of being retained. The only modification made to the Shared Journal process was the elimination of the negotiation and voting. This modification was made to shorten the process due to the time constraints of the pull-out intervention program. Typically, two students volunteered to share a story about important events from their lives. The other students asked questions to clarify and obtain additional information, then the students were able to write about one of the shared stories. They could choose which story to include in their journals. Interestingly, the students often informally negotiated so that they were all writing about the same topic. It began to be important to them that they "share" the story.

As with the other intervention group, these students improved in their literacy abilities as well as their attitudes and willingness to participate and take risks. The students began to use "more highly developed sentence structures, more conventional spellings, more invented spellings which approached convention, and longer, more detailed stories" (Gunnels, 1992, p. 100). One example of the progress made by the children is from Jackie. She initially wrote three to five lines of print and an illustration. One of her early entries follows.

> I was lug [looking] it [at] TV in [and] I hrt [heard] a fiy-chuk [fire truck] ni [and] the Pr rmigis [paramedics] thes [they] was at a pitn [building] I wit [went] in the bik [back] yrt [yard] in [and] I Luk [look] it [out] uv [of] My KiPin [kitchen] wuthr [window]

As the intervention program continued, Jackie spent more time writing and less time completing illustrations. Occasionally, her entries would continue for several pages. One of her later entries is below.

> [*Page 1*] My Mom hif to go to The did [doctor] in [and] she yos [was] too take sus [us] up My eny [auntie] hise [house] in [and] my eny tod [told] us to

> trn [turn] the trnDow [Nintendo] of [off] in [and] prt [point] m [her] fag [finger] to us in [*Page 2*] tod [told] us to kum in the frut [front] run [room] ni [and] tod us to sut [sit] din [down] on the flr [floor] in My Buth [brother] sid [sit] un [on] the sofr [sofa] in she tod him too git on the flr [floor] in she [*Page 3*] git [got] the most tol [remote control] in ol moth [almost] hit him

Jackie's writings included many conventionally spelled words. Her invented spellings included many conventionally represented phonemes. She also began to make corrections in her own writings as she read her journal entries to the teacher and her peers. Her self-corrections were invaluable in helping her continue to progress.

The researcher found that, in this study, the ability to experience success was essential to children's literacy acquisition. Shared Journal provided opportunities for them to share stories from their lives and have those stories respected and valued. The children initially saw reading and writing as dreaded tasks rather than enjoyable activities. At the end of the intervention, they were eager to share their stories and to record their own stories as well as the stories from their peers in their journals. They also all felt that the sharing of their stories was important. They didn't get upset if the other children chose not to write about their stories. Instead, it was the sharing of their stories that was most important because it allowed their voices to be heard.

Shared Journal also provided opportunities for these students to experience success and to serve as "teachers" with their peers. This was seldom the case for them in the regular classrooms since they were at risk of failure in first grade. As the children were writing their story, the following occurred.

Jarard	Katherine, how you spell yo name?
Katherine	K-A-T-H-E-R-I-N-E.
Jarard	How you spell "and"? [directed to the group]
Tosha	A-N-D.
Cedric	How you know?
Tosha	Cause "N" go n-n-n [sounding out]. Katherine sister fell and, wait… bumped she head.
Jackie	Bumped. B-… what else?
Katherine	Dat "B" is backwards.
Jackie	Oh. [erases and corrects]
Jarard	Katherine's sister, um, tried a cartwheel. She bumped her head on a tree… what is it now? Right here.
Katherine	Tree *stump*. Yeah. Stump. You make it like this. [She proceeds to draw a tree stump.]

During this collaboration, the children provided and received assistance with the spellings of several words, clarification of events in the shared story, letter-sound correspondences, directionality of letters, and ideas for illustrations. They were all able to seek assistance as well as serve as teachers.

Shared Journal in Preschool Settings

Shared Journal has been effectively used in several preschool settings. The reason that it is so successful with very young children is that it builds on their need for conversation, authentic language experiences, and their love of stories. It also addresses the preschool teachers' objectives for group time. The keys to using Shared Journal with very young children are to accept children's spelling approximations, avoid using direct skill-drill teaching during Shared Journal, and value or celebrate the children's approximations.

The oral sharing step of Shared Journal helps the preschoolers build community, feel that they belong to the group, and creates a need to know about others, which allows for authentic discussions of real dilemmas. It challenges the very young child's egocentric view of the world by making others' stories interesting enough to listen to and talk about. For example, when Mallory shared about crying when she went to the circus with her grandmother, Soren wanted to know why she cried. When she replied that the clowns scared her, he blurted out that she didn't need to be afraid. Her grandmother could keep her safe like his did when he went.

The voting step of Shared Journal helps the very young children see a need for counting, using numbers, and being accurate with their counting. It also helps them with making decisions. For example, on one occasion, Kristen was the Community Helper who helped with vote counting. Her friends were most concerned for her because she didn't practice accuracy when counting. Three of her friends spent some of their Center Time helping her with counting to make sure she did it correctly.

The writing step of Shared Journal helps very young children want to draw and write so that their classmates can read their stories. They love to have others talk to them about their drawings or "letters that they used in their words." Many begin their written representations with scribbles. This is exemplified by the arrival of a new, just turning four-year-old. After the young child experienced Shared Journal for the first time, R.J., an older four-year-old, explained that it was okay for Brandon to "scribble scrabble" "... cause he's just a baby."

The Shared Journal process should be modified for the preschool classroom. Teachers use a "marker" to designate where each child sits in the circle. Some teachers use a carpet piece or a laminated picture of each child that is cut into a mat so that the children know where they sit. The use of a circle for a seating arrangement is most important for the preschool children as it allows them to see the storyteller and "stay in their space." Teachers limit the number who share each day but do not assign specific days for specific children. When the teacher assigns a day for a child to share, then the parent or guardian may feel pressured to buy something or do something so that the child has something to share. By having the children decide when and what they share, they begin to realize that they have events in their lives that others will find interesting. Teachers also often use a timer so that children can see how long they have for telling their stories. This visible reminder helps them shape the story. If this is not done, young children will talk and talk because they love the being the center of attention. The timer is also used during the question/answer session so that the children begin to realize that they need to ask questions about the storyteller's story not use that time to tell their own stories. (Even though the timer is used, the children are allowed to vote if they feel the storyteller or the group needs more time.)

The children are allowed to use props (e.g. stuffed toy, truck, program from the circus, menu) during their sharing. The prop often helps them remember what they want to share and keeps other children interested. The teacher must use caution with the use of props so that the children do not begin to try to outdo other storytellers. After the sharing, the children vote; this voting is more formality than anything. They often vote for one story and then write and draw about another story. At this young age, teachers allow this because of the developmental level of the children. Within several months of using Shared Journal each day, very young children are often drawing representational pictures, using invented spellings and some conventional spellings, and reading their stories/representations to others.

Summary

Shared Journal, when used with special groups of students like those examined in this chapter, can produce amazing results. Teachers often use the Shared Journal process as described in Chapter 2 with little or no modifications. If needed, however, modifications can be made, such as limiting the number of students sharing, having the teacher assist by rephrasing what is shared, or eliminating the need for negotiation and voting. One of the best qualities of Shared Journal is that it provides many options for adapting to fit the needs of the teacher and the students. The benefits, even in modified models, include both academic and socio-emotional development. For these special groups of children, this kind of opportunity is invaluable.

eleven
Assessment and Documentation

A Teacher's Story

Teachers are under tremendous pressure due to legislation and mandates requiring that they be accountable for documenting and assessing students' learning in a systematic manner to demonstrate adequate progress. Assessment is also a critical element of a balanced instructional system. It provides teachers with a systematic opportunity to look at children's cognitive strategies rather than their scores on a worksheet or standardized test. By focusing on strategies rather than students' wrong answers, teachers are able to address the core of each student's learning. It also allows teachers to revise teaching strategies to meet students' needs.

Shared Journal is ideal for documenting and assessing whole class and individual student progress. The daily process allows teachers to monitor individual abilities to tell stories, ask questions, share concerns and ideas, and to record a version of the story based on their understandings of reading, writing, and drawing. In addition, it offers teachers the opportunity to assess students' understandings of history, mathematics, science, and social studies, as well as the social development of community among the students. Teachers can also combine the individual assessments to provide documentation of whole-class progress. Teachers carry out this documentation and assessment in a variety of ways. A classroom teacher, Angela Carr, shares her approach to documentation and assessment in this chapter. Although the chapter focuses on Angela's approaches to documenting students' progress, informing others about that progress, and evaluating teaching methods, these approaches are culturally and developmentally appropriate, and thus can be modified to fit other teachers' needs.

Documenting Students' Progress

Students come to us with varying developmental and ability levels. We must first identify where each child is in his development before we can move him forward. I begin with evaluation of writing development using the Writing Development Checklist that is shown below (see Table 11.1). It is used to monitor writing development from the time a child picks up a pencil until he/she can write conventionally. This checklist was created using the writing stages established by Kamii and Manning (2002) as documented in Chapter 3 of this book.

Shortly after the first week of school, I take a journal sample from each student's journal. I do not do this on the first day because young children are often too intimidated

TABLE 11.1 Writing Development Checklist

	Aug.	Oct.	Dec.	Mar.	May
Stage 1 Writes with pictures					
Stage 2 Scribbles for monster					
Stage 3 Letter stringing—no sound symbol correspondence *Dklgktkdjd* for monster					
Stage 4 Use of an initial consonant to represent an entire word *M* for monster					
Stage 5 Initial and final consonants serve as word boundaries *MR* for monster					
Stage 6 Inclusion of medial consonant; awareness of blends; may divide blend *MSTR* for monster					
Stage 7 Initial, final, and medial consonants and vowel placeholder. Vowel is incorrect. Does not space between words. *Mestrrscre* for Monsters are scary.					
Stage 8 Initial, final, and medial consonants and vowel placeholder. Some vowels are correct. Spaces between words. *Monstrs r skere* for Monsters are scary.					
Stage 9 Conventional spelling *Monsters are scary.*					

to write independently. It takes a week or so for many of them to feel comfortable taking a risk with writing. Once I have collected a journal writing sample, I document the writing stage by placing an X in the appropriate box under August on the writing checklist. A sample is taken every grading period to document progress. I keep the checklist and writing samples in the Writing section of their portfolio. Students move through stages of writing at different times and at different rates. The checklist shows growth over an extended period of time.

This writing checklist is also used to document how the class is doing as a whole at any given time during the school year. This is done by plotting an "X" for each student on a master checklist on a given date. For example, if Johnny is at stage 2 on October 1st, an X is placed in Stage 2. If Mary is in Stage 3, an X is placed in Stage 3, and so on. This continues until all children have been placed on the master checklist, allowing the teacher to provide whole-class documentation of levels on a given date. This informs the classroom teacher, as well as the administrator, of the overall developmental level of the students in the class. By documenting this information several times throughout the year, teachers can see the growth the class has made. Likewise, teachers are able to see students who are not moving and not showing progress over time. This information is valuable in family–teacher conferences. When I meet with families, I use the checklists to show students' growth. If the student is struggling to make progress, I show the family the next writing stage to which we are working. This gives both me and the family an attainable goal to work towards without the stigma of defeat or failure.

My school requires that we have monthly meetings to examine data related to student progress. During our monthly data meetings I meet with the school reading specialist and administrator to discuss reading test performance. Here, I relate the students' reading development to their writing development. For example, if a student is struggling with vowel sounds in her reading, it is likely that she is struggling with them in her writing. If this is the case, I focus on helping the student "hear" the vowel sound as she says it and focus on the print as she is writing. By writing and reading the spoken sound simultaneously the student progresses at a faster rate than if just practicing reading a text.

Special education teachers work collaboratively with classroom teachers. The checklist and journal samples help the teachers devise an intervention plan. For example, if the student is consistently representing a word by using only the initial sound, the teachers discuss strategies for helping the student hear the other sounds in the words. These strategies might include having the student label his illustration. When a student sees the illustration of the objects on his paper with just one letter beside each of them, if he has developed the minimum-maximum hypothesis, he recognizes that a single letter is not enough to represent that object. It is more difficult for the student to recognize this when he is writing a string of letters on his paper to represent an entire story.

Assessment Informs Teaching and Learning

The journal entry is a daily picture of where the child is in the writing process. Because students are at varying developmental and ability levels, individualized instruction is necessary and is implemented through daily interaction and intervention. The assessment truly becomes meaningful when teachers make decisions about how they are going to help students advance toward the next level. Teachers interact as editors and models, using the information from the assessment.

Teacher as Reader and Editor

Every day the teacher reads each child's journal entry. She serves as a reader when reading the story for enjoyment and as an editor when conferencing with each student. This is a brief (e.g. two to ten minutes at the most) but meaningful interaction. My level of interaction and editing is student-specific. Just as no two journal entries are the same, my comments and interactions are not the same with each student. As the students share their entries with me, I try to find one or two specific things to comment on to help challenge their thinking. For example, if one student shares an entry that just has a picture on it, I may challenge her by saying, "I can see you drew a picture about the story. Could you put some writing with your picture?" This question will cause the child to consider the difference between drawing and writing, as well as encouraging her to go a step further. Likewise, if a student is struggling with a specific skill throughout his entry, such as the use of punctuation, this is the focus of the conference. For example, if a student shares an entry that has no punctuation, I would challenge him by asking, "Where does your sentence stop? How can you let others know it stops there?" My conferencing is specific to the child. Some conferences may last a minute while others may last four minutes. None lasts over ten minutes. The students work at their tables. I work with individuals or a small group of students who are working at the same writing skill level. As the other students finish, they bring their journals to me and we conference. This is as informal and brief as possible, as I want this to be their journal, not mine. I do not want them to lose ownership of their writing.

Here is a sample from Haley, a kindergarten student, who was struggling with "ch" and "sh" in her writing:

December 1, 2008

Virginia wet to shuke sheses [Chuck E. Cheese] she plad lots uv gams [games] ad [and] she at pesu [pizza] and kak sh [she] sol [saw] suke [Chuck E.] wan [when] see [she] was dun [done] she plad mor.

In this entry "sh" was used instead of "ch" on three occasions. She also used "se" instead of "sh" once.

The student and I talked about the difference between "ch" and "sh" after she read the entry to me. I also pointed out how she had spelled "she" using the correct sounds several times as well as her error when she spelled it as "see." Haley went back to her seat, made the changes I had suggested, and read the entry to me again.

A few days later another child shared about going to Chuck E. Cheese. I could immediately tell that my conference with Haley just a few days prior was a success since she used "ch" correctly in one word in the following entry.

December 4, 2008

Cassie wet to Chuke sheses she at shes cak se plad lots of gams she is sex [six]

In this entry Haley substituted "sh" for "ch" in one word and "se" for "sh" in another. I pointed these out to her while reading her entry. Again, she made the corrections I suggested.

Three months later, another Chuck E. Cheese story was shared. Haley had written several entries that had the "ch" and "sh" sounds in them between December and March. Each time I would correct her briefly, and she would make changes. Our conferences helped Haley hear and write these sounds correctly. Haley's entry follows:

March 3, 2009

Virginia wit to chuke chis she got a gren [green] wrm [worm] she liks [likes] it.

There were no "sh" or "ch" errors in this entry. I praised Haley about her proper use of "ch" and "sh" in her entry. In my classroom, praise comes with a "happy dance." I jump up and do a short dance and then announce to the class what the student has accomplished. I then make a copy of this milestone to keep in her portfolio. When the celebration subsides we turn our attention back to the journal. For Haley, I asked her to go to the sight word chart to find the words "like" and "went" and correct those in her journal. Our sight word chart is a chart of words that the students are learning to read in isolation. As a part of our reading program, the students are introduced to two words per week. The chart hangs at the front of the room, and we use it as a reference in our writing.

Teacher editing is not meant to correct all of the errors students have in their entries. Instead, it is a tool that is used to help students grow and develop their writing skills. Therefore, teachers must conference with the students in a way that communicates to them that we are their coach, not their critic. Students quickly understand that editing is the norm and that they will be expected to change or add to their entry each day after sharing it with the teacher. This interaction communicates to the student that we can always make small changes to make our writing better and easier for our audience to read.

Teacher as Model

Teacher modeling is critical in Shared Journal. This modeling occurs in the sharing and negotiation phase of Shared Journal as well as the actual writing process. When teachers share their own stories, they foster students' interest in stories. As active members of the group during sharing time, they ask questions and make comments about the students' stories. As teachers and students begin using Shared Journal, teachers need to model during negotiation. This is a crucial time for modeling. The teacher can help the students understand the need to listen to others' points of view by being an active listener who restates what she hears the speaker say. She also models turn taking by allowing and encouraging students to offer their opinions. Finally, she helps the students draw conclusions by summing up what she has heard. When the teacher has been an active participant and facilitator in negotiation at the beginning of the year, students become more independent in their thinking. They begin to offer their reasons for selecting a story. For example, when Weston was called on to negotiate, he said, "We should write about the cat story because Natalee told us ALL about that cat. Taylor didn't tell us much about his t-ball game." This comment shows that the students are beginning to focus on what makes a good story. Rubrics can be developed to document and assess students' growth in reasoning and presenting an argument.

Teachers' modeling during the writing process is critical to the development of students' writing. Students must construct sound symbol correspondences before they can move through the writing stages. Traditionally, letters and sounds are taught in isolation in a sequential manner over an extended period of time. Shared Journal creates an authentic purpose for the students to master sound symbol correspondences at a much faster pace. This requires the teacher to intervene and model the process for students. Many students master this right away using an alphabet chart as a guide, while others require more support. I always require that all students "write" in their journal independently before asking for help so that I can see a true picture of where they are in their development and to keep them from being dependent upon me. I then ask them what they would like to add to their entries and help them sound out the words on their papers, focusing on phonetic spelling, not conventional spelling. By focusing on phonetic spelling, students begin to see themselves as authors. They are free to take risks and be successful without the fear of their writing not being "right." As the students become more accomplished in reading, I begin to help them make the connection between their writing and conventional spelling.

Once students are comfortable with sounding out words on their own and recording these sounds on their paper, I help them move to separating the strings of letters into words. I do this by asking the students what they would like to write. Then we count the words on our fingers as the student says them, and I write that many blanks on the paper. They write the words as I help them focus on the spaces.

These two examples of modeling show how teacher interaction changes as the students grow and make progress in their writing. The modeling begins to help students understand the link between spoken and written language and gradually moves into focusing on the student as a storyteller. Students may be at the same level on the writing development checklist but at varying levels on the development of the narrative itself. This is true in both oral and written narratives.

The rubric shown as Table 11.2 was created to show points to consider when teachers evaluate personal narratives (McCabe & Bliss, 2003; Miranda, McCabe, & Bliss, 1998). These components can be tracked in the oral and written steps in Shared Journal over time.

Often, teachers are interested in the children's development of stories, but they do not know how to document growth. McCabe and Bliss (2003) as well as Miranda, McCabe, and Bliss (1998) have identified eight general structures for narratives. These structures help teachers identify the developmental levels of the students' stories as well as decide what strategies could help advance the students' thinking about stories. Table 11.3 shows a checklist created using these structures to track oral or written narrative development. These rubrics can be used with all ages of students. For the beginning of kindergarten, it is best used for oral narrative development. As the year progresses, teachers can shift to using it to assess written narratives. The teacher can track individual students' progress as well as the class as a whole. This will enable the teacher to provide guidance and modeling in specific areas.

Grading

Teachers of elementary-aged students are often required by administrators to keep grade books. Because Shared Journal is done on a daily basis, it is an avenue for teachers to assess students' progress and development over time. The intent is to look at the students' body of work to assess their progress; it is not to grade individual entries. If necessary,

TABLE 11.2 Components of a Narrative Rubric

	Aug.	Oct.	Dec.	May
1 = Incomplete 2 = Beginning to experiment with 3 = Using 4 = Highly developed story				
Topic Maintenance The number of sentences, statements, facts offered about a central theme or topic. Does the student maintain focus on the topic?				
Information Provided The completeness of information about the narrative and events within that narrative who, what, when, where				
Event Sequencing The use of chronological ordering of events or some other order that is logical and acceptable to the group (flashback)				
Referencing Identifying people, places and events				
Use of conjunctions Phrases or clauses that link details or events				
Fluency How the narrative flows Voice, tone, expression				

teachers can use checklists and forms to analyze and evaluate student progress and derive a grade for various content areas. For example, the checklist shown as Table 11.4 can be used to grade the writing of more advanced students. This checklist allows teachers to look at authentic writing samples versus testing the skills in isolation. The checklists in this chapter encompass multiple aspects of writing. Teachers can analyze what is being written as well as how the students are writing it. Both grammar and composition can be assessed at every grade level.

Anecdotal Records

One of the most powerful assessment tools to use with Shared Journal is the anecdotal record. Teachers observe learning in all subject areas during the Shared Journal process. In my classroom, the student who is recording questions and comments will announce how many more questions and comments are remaining. This illustrates the students' understanding of number. Peers will correct one another during sharing with comments like, "You asked a question. The questions have all been asked already." A student who

TABLE 11.3 Narrative Development Rubric

Narrative Development	Date	Date	Date	Date
One Event Narrative One event or action told in past tense, e.g. "I ate ice cream."				
Two Event Narrative Story has two events, e.g. "I ate ice cream with my grandmother."				
Miscellaneous Narrative Contains more than two past tense actions or events but without logical or causal sequence/order.				
Leap-Frog Narrative Includes events that are not sequenced or omits major events so that the listener/reader must infer a logical causal sequence and must infer the omitted events.				
Chronological Narrative Contains the chronological sequence of events but without much coherence so that the story sounds like a travel itinerary.				
End at the High Point Narrative Builds to the high point and ends abruptly without any resolution or closing.				
Classic Narrative Narrator orients the listener/reader to who, what, when, where something occurred, builds action to the high point and provides resolution.				

goes to the map to show where he/she went on vacation while another student comments on whether the student traveled North, South, East or West illustrates an understanding or lack of understanding of geography. Children who share stories that always happened "yesterday" or "another day" help teachers pinpoint their limited understanding of time. In contrast, students who figure out the number pattern on the calendar will often work ahead and date the pages for their journal for the whole month. This shows a deeper understanding of number and time. These are all examples of how children are learning so much more than reading and writing during Shared Journal.

By making notes during Shared Journal, a teacher gathers information that helps her understand the developmental level of the whole child. I use mailing labels on a clipboard to record student comments and teacher observations. Each child has an anecdotal page in his or her portfolio. I transfer these labels to their anecdotal page to aid in assessing other areas of the curriculum.

TABLE 11.4 Journal Writing Checklist

Skills Assessed	Score	Comments
States the main idea		
Includes supporting details		
Uses adjectives		
Uses transition words: and, but, first, next		
Uses complete sentences		
Uses compound sentences		
Uses complex sentences		
Capital letters		
Periods		
Spells sight words correctly		
Apostrophe s to show possession		
Contractions		
Exclamation points		
Quotation marks		
Uses correct verb tense		

Score code

\+ Applied skill throughout writing (10 points) Points possible _____

✓ Beginning to apply skill (5 points)

– Did not apply skill (0 points) Points earned_____

N Not applicable on this journal entry

Grade _____%

Assessing Other Areas of the Curriculum

Shared Journal offers teachers opportunities to assess other areas of the curriculum as well as writing and storytelling. In my view, Shared Journal serves as one tool for assessment of history, social studies, science, and math. Teachers may want to use it along with other means of assessment. I offer the following suggestions for using Shared Journal to assess history, social studies, science, and math. These ideas are compiled from conversations with other teachers who have used Shared Journal for assessment in those areas.

One idea is to use a rubric that addresses the tools that historians use. For example, the rubric would include whether the child is able to pose questions and define terms; whether the child uses different types of questions and how many were posed; whether the child uses the information about details from the stories in his writing; whether the child uses the information simply as a restating of the facts or a synthesis of them; how the child uses and understands notions of time; and how he reports/tells the other child's story (e.g. accuracy, using the story as a springboard for a further story or discussion). The following are examples of two children's efforts to understand war. These entries came after one of their classmates shared about his father being sent to Iraq.

Entry 1—War Definition

I think we should not have war because I do not want any of our soldiers to get hurt. I do not want any of the soldiers' families to worry about them. I am glad that they are fighting for me. They are very brave because they are going to the Middle East and fighting for us. I know they miss their families. I know they hate sleeping in the tents at night. I know they miss their home-made meal. I wish we did not have war.

Entry 2—War Definition

I have seen some things on TV and I hope that you have a TV. I did not watch the TV today. If some of the soldiers die the women will not be able to have husbands and it the soldiers kids will not be able to have their daddys and if the men do not die the women and kids will be able to have their husbands and daddys.

Both of these entries document the children's understanding of war. Because the teacher was assessing social studies and history, she did not focus on writing or spelling development. For this assessment, she focused on the content and meaning of the entries. She was able to provide evidence that the children could explain the concept of "war" and give details to support their explanation. Although neither child retold the storyteller's story, both focused on their concerns about what happens to people in wars.

Shared Journal serves as a beginning point for many math, social studies, and science projects. Topics shared often encourage the germination of ideas for these projects. When teachers attend to these teachable moments, they incorporate these topics into their social studies and science curriculum. The curriculum is more authentic and meaningful to the children because their voices were heard and used. A checklist helps teachers record and examine the children's ideas. Each teacher could modify the checklist to fit her children's needs, as well as the standards that she must ensure her children meet by the year's end. The checklist could include the following:

1. How children clarified the idea for a project based on the sharing and writing in Shared Journal.
2. How children described their ideas and thoughts about procedures for the project.
3. Whether the children categorized key points.
4. Whether children considered the time factor for the project.
5. Whether children understood and focused on the problem.
6. How fair the children were with each other as they discussed.

When children get ideas for projects from stories that have been shared, teachers can document this. For example, when a child shared that his cousin was in the hospital because she was having treatments for cancer, the children not only wrote about this story but also decided to make a quilt for her so that she could know how much they cared. Making the quilt turned into a class project that then became part of a theme on friendship. A rubric would document and assess the social studies standards for this project.

The easiest way to assess math, science, and social studies is with the use of a master checklist that has the standards for the school year listed across the top of the checklist and the children's names listed down the side. As the teacher hears children discuss various topics (e.g. community helpers), aspects of this discussion (e.g. vocabulary about various community helpers) can be noted on the checklist. This checklist can be used to document children's development. It can also be used for teaching purposes as it allows the teacher to easily see the class development as a whole. She can form groups for mini-lessons based on observations of need from the checklist. In addition, she can keep track of the curriculum requirements, making certain that all areas are addressed. Finally, she can use the checklist to address accountability issues with administrators.

Summary

Shared Journal provides an authentic environment for teachers to assess students' development and learning. Assessment is not separate from instruction. Instead, it is what happens each time a teacher interacts with a student, draws conclusions, and acts upon those conclusions. Over time, Shared Journal provides an in-depth knowledge of students' progress and development in all aspects of the curriculum.

twelve
Teachers as Advocates

Teachers are constantly seeking new methods that meet required mandates, standards, and tests to help their students learn. They search out and implement different strategies so that their students will be successful in all academic areas. As teachers incorporate ideas and practices, they continuously question, research, and evaluate their effectiveness. In addition, they need to help others understand what they are doing and why they are doing it. This chapter will address how teachers can effectively advocate for Shared Journal.

Advocating with Self and Other Teachers

Once teachers implement Shared Journal and begin to see the progress of their students, they will want to advocate for the use of this process. A simple way to begin showing other teachers about Shared Journal is to display samples of the children's journal entries. When other teachers see what the children are doing, they may begin to ask questions. How did you get the children to begin writing? How do you get the children to stay on task while they are working in their journals? How do you get the children to take time with their illustrations? Are the children actively engaged in the storytelling and questioning? How do you find time to include this in your schedule? How do I get started with this process? What do the parents think of Shared Journal? Sharing more student work samples will build on the validity of Shared Journal. Also, allowing students to visit other classrooms to share their journal entries and celebrate their successes is an excellent way to show others the progress of the students. In addition, teachers should volunteer to assist other teachers in beginning Shared Journal in their classrooms. Teachers can provide workshops or training sessions for those colleagues who are interested in the implementation of Shared Journal. Being available to answer questions and assist with the process are ways to help other teachers try this strategy and begin a school-wide implementation of Shared Journal.

Preparation and Time

When considering any new strategy, teachers always have questions related to the preparation and time needed to implement the process. Some teachers struggle with adding a new process to their already overloaded curriculum. Teachers can be reassured that, with Shared Journal, the preparation time is minimal. Preparing the journals for each month is all that is required in order to be ready for implementation. The time allotted for Shared Journal depends on the teacher's schedule and the age of the students. The whole process (sharing, discussing/negotiating, voting, and journal entry) may be completed in one time frame. However, the method is flexible, and the sharing, discussing/negotiating, and voting may be completed in one time period with the completion of the journal entry during another time.

Teachers can make time for Shared Journal, as it incorporates required standards and mandates and thus, it can replace the teaching of isolated skills. For example, Shared Journal is an excellent way to help young children learn how to ask questions. In the beginning, children do not know the difference between a question and a statement. When the teacher asks for questions, young children raise their hands and make statements. As they begin to see a need to get information for their journal entry, they start asking who, what, when, where, and why questions. Older children learn to refine their questions so that they get the details of the story that will make their version particularly interesting and effective. Through modeling by the teacher and the students' need to gather information, the ability to ask questions comes easily to the students.

Students' Sharing

At first, teachers may be anxious about students' sharing. Sometimes teachers say, "What if they do not have a story to share?" Students of all ages come to school with stories to tell others. Most children are eager to share their experiences with all who will listen, including their teachers and peers. Teachers who listen and establish relationships with their students will always have stories for sharing. Through establishing these relationships, teachers will be able to help those children who are shy and do not initially share their experiences with others. It is the responsibility of the teacher to initiate conversation with those students. Through these conversations, the teacher can assist a student in sharing experiences with their classmates.

For example, Andrea was a very shy kindergarten student. She never shared her personal experiences with the teacher or other classmates. In fact, she interacted very little with others. One morning, Andrea walked into the classroom and was wearing a new dress. This was unusual for her. The teacher walked over to Andrea and began talking about her dress. As the teacher complimented her on the dress, Andrea beamed with pleasure. During the sharing of stories, the teacher volunteered Andrea's story about the new dress. As the children asked questions, the teacher assisted her with the answers. Andrea's story was selected for the journal entry, and she seemed to enjoy listening to her peers as they worked in their journals on her story. From this point forward, Andrea began sharing personal experiences with the teacher and became more confident in her abilities to share her stories with her classmates.

Teachers' screening of stories with individual students helps in making sure the stories are appropriate and acceptable for class discussion. Teachers often encounter two issues with this process. First, teachers may not see a need to screen children's journal topics. When screening is omitted, teachers often face situations where children share inappropriate information. For example, when one student Polly stood up to share, she told about being locked in the closet and watching through the keyhole as her parents smoked crack. The second issue occurs when the teacher screens the story, but the student decides to make the story more interesting by changing it. For example, Bobby told his teacher he wanted to share about a birthday party, but when he stood up to share, he told about his father hitting his mother. While these stories are important for the teacher to hear, care needs to be taken that they are not shared with the entire class. Helping students understand that there are private and public stories that we share, and with whom we share them, is important.

Students' Emotions

Teachers question how to handle students' emotions after voting. If the teacher values the oral sharing as much as the written entry, then children will also value the opportunity to share their stories. Some teachers use a graph where children record the number of times they share so that all class members can keep up with it. The graph is then used by the children to discuss which story should be selected, based on the number of times students have shared.

Some children may feel hurt because their stories were not selected. Teachers have to make sure that the focus is on the story and not the child. Using the title or key words about the content of the story rather than the name of the student helps with this focus on the story. Also, it helps to have at least three students sharing stories so as to not have a winner and loser. In addition, it is the responsibility of the teacher to keep track of the stories in the journals to make sure all students are included within a reasonable length of time. This record of journal entries can also serve as another tool to help students reason about and decide on the journal entry. These discussions assist students as they begin to think about and understand the feelings of others.

Classroom Community

Teachers worry about how the children will learn to get along with each other when they come from diverse backgrounds. However, as children participate in Shared Journal, they come to know each other in ways that are not possible in any other curriculum. Through the daily sharing, students learn many things about themselves and their peers. They see that they share similar experiences and have many of the same feelings. As they identify with one another, they begin to establish bonds and connections with their peers. This is very important in helping students develop a community of learners in the classroom. Also, during discussions, students have opportunities to share their thoughts and opinions. Over time, the students are able to talk about why a topic is worthy of selection and why another student wants to have his story in the journal. They begin to take the perspective of another student. Beginning to consider the viewpoints of others is a very important benefit of Shared Journal.

Meeting Standards

In all school districts, teachers are concerned with meeting academic standards. They may question how Shared Journal will meet those standards. This process incorporates the communicative arts—listening, speaking, reading, writing, and viewing. Teachers can share their grids (similar to that shown in Table 8.1 in Chapter 8) to explain how the standards are met. Students learn how to tell stories to an audience and, in turn, learn how to be a part of an audience through careful listening. Students have to listen in order to get information and to know what questions have been asked. Also, students have to speak in a clear and loud tone in order to be understood by others. Reading and writing go hand in hand in the journal entry. The written text and the illustration indicate the student's comprehension of the story. The written text also shows the teacher the student's level in phonological and literacy development. The information related to student knowledge and development is much greater in the daily journal entry than on a worksheet, where students simply have to make a selection as the answer.

Most school districts require students in the elementary grades to participate in state testing. Many early childhood grades test their students using different evaluation instruments. These assessment tools evaluate many components, such as the student's ability to identify phonemes, recognize letters, segment the phonemes in words, and read words. Some assessments require students to read nonsense words. Participation in Shared Journal provides students with daily opportunities to segment words, and this includes beginning, middle, and ending sounds. Also, in writing the text for the daily entry, students get ample practice in recognizing and writing letters and in blending sounds and reading words. Shared Journal prepares students to be successful with assessment items related to literacy.

Advocating with Families and Community Members

Teachers need to introduce Shared Journal to families and community members as well as educate them to its benefits. Helping them understand and appreciate Shared Journal will go a long way toward securing their support. There are many ways to help parents and others understand Shared Journal.

In the beginning of the process, letters may be sent home or to community leaders to explain Shared Journal. These letters communicate to others the steps involved in Shared Journal, the goals for the children, what can be expected in regard to the children's progress, and how to interact and facilitate the experience outside of the classroom.

Open House and Curriculum Nights are also venues for educating others about Shared Journal. During these sessions, teachers can help families understand that children do not have to bring items to school to share with their peers but may share their life experiences. Teachers must explain that the stories in the journals are about actual events that children experience. Children enjoy talking about playing with their friends, attending a birthday party, or spending an afternoon at grandmother's house. These events are of interest to their peers because the experiences are real and, most of the time, have occurred in the lives of the other children. This creates interest among the children and a strong desire to participate in Shared Journal.

In addition, teachers help families and community leaders understand how the actual journal entry shows the academic progress of the child. The illustrations and text within the journal indicate a student's level of development and progress. Teachers should discuss the importance of details in the illustrations and in the texts. For example, details included in the picture and text are indications of the child's comprehension of the story. The written text shows where the child is in his development. Through the writings, parents are able to follow the children's progress as they move toward the goals of reading and writing. In addition, teachers may inform families of young children that a child's developmental spelling demonstrates his knowledge and understanding of letters, the sounds the letters represent, and how to combine the letters to express thoughts in text. The teacher's goal is to help families understand that allowing children to write at their developmental levels will provide an environment that promotes confidence and independence. As their writing abilities increase, they begin naturally to move toward using writing conventions.

Advocating with Administrators and Policy Makers

Administrators and policy makers are always concerned with academic standards and student achievement. As stated previously, Shared Journal addresses academic standards. All communicative arts are incorporated in the process, as well as other areas of the curriculum. In addition, higher level skills, such as questioning and composition, are daily staples. Shared Journal provides an excellent process for documentation to demonstrate student progress and achievement.

As with other teachers and families, a good public relations plan will help in educating administrators and policy makers. Displaying student work samples outside of the classroom is a simple and nonthreatening way to show student abilities. Also, having children share their journal entries with administrators can be very convincing. If appropriate, teachers may allow their children to take their journals to the administrative office in the school and share their entries with office personnel and administrators. In addition, school administrators may be invited to visit the classroom to observe Shared Journal and celebrate the children's journal entries. Having the children discuss and read their stories can be instrumental in demonstrating the positive effects of Shared Journal to administrators and others.

Establishing relationships with school leaders (e.g. school board members, PTA officers, community stakeholders) can be helpful in furthering the support of administrators. It is important to keep in mind the focus of school administrators and policy makers. Teachers need to focus on administrators' goals as they provide interactions with students and share students' work. For example, if a journal entry is about a community event or board members reading to the class, these would be excellent choices to share with these leaders.

It may be the case that administrators will allow teachers to use Shared Journal, but also require the use of textbooks or specific curriculum components. Teachers should not be discouraged by this. When this happens, teachers can evaluate their requirements and schedule in order to determine how they can implement Shared Journal. One strategy could be to divide the Shared Journal process so that large group sharing is incorporated with other large group activities. For example, the sharing of events may be included as part of large group activities that focus on language arts. Activities that stress listening and speaking will work well with the sharing and questioning of events. Also, the discussion and negotiation are venues for children to reason and persuade others to see their points of view. The illustrating and writing may be included with other small group activities or literacy centers. Defining time in the schedule for children to share events from their lives and then documenting these experiences will prove to be rewarding and beneficial to the development and achievement of the children.

When teachers present reasons for implementing Shared Journal in their classroom, they must identify the benefits. They must also explain how those benefits support the mission of the school and the goals of the administrator. Teachers may mention that

Shared Journal is cost effective, involves little preparation time, and is flexible with scheduling. Also, Shared Journal prepares students for state testing and continuously develops academic standards that include all communicative arts components, the concept of story, questioning, perspective taking, and social development, as well as other content areas. Helping students be successful both in the classroom and in society are goals of all teachers, and Shared Journal provides an avenue for meeting these goals.

Administrators as Advocates for Using Shared Journal

Administrators can serve as advocates for the use of Shared Journal in their schools. We have found that schools where administrators actively support Shared Journal are the most successful. If administrators have an understanding and thorough knowledge of Shared Journal, they, in turn, become supporters of the process. Administrators' support is multifaceted, ongoing, and tailored to meet the needs of the children and their families, as well as the teachers and staff. It includes understanding the Shared Journal process, reading what has been written about it, listening to teachers who used it, and being able to discuss it with others. This support is crucial to teachers who are implementing new teaching strategies. In addition, providing inservice opportunities to teachers is another way that administrators may assist teachers with the implementation of Shared Journal.

There are many opportunities for administrators to help educate families, policy makers, and community members about Shared Journal. They can host Open House events for school officials, elected officials in the community, and families. During these events, they can talk about the benefits of Shared Journal, discuss the importance of Shared Journal to the school's literacy program, and present students' journals as evidence of academic progress. Having teachers and additional instructional staff members participate in these stakeholder sessions will help in educating others about Shared Journal.

Administrators can ask teachers to conduct multiple educational sessions for staff, district employees, and families. At these workshops, teachers can conduct presentations to explain Shared Journal. Providing samples of students' work will give additional information regarding how Shared Journal meets the academic goals, objectives, and standards of the school. Providing Question and Answer sessions allows others to ask specific questions and gives teachers an opportunity to discuss different points of interest and provide more examples to support the implementation of Shared Journal in the classroom.

As with any new program, administrators must be aware of the impact change has on teachers, children, and families. Craine (2007) and others (Hall & Loucks, 1979; Hord, Rutherford, Huling-Austin, & Hall, 1987) explain that it is natural for people to resist change. They go through a cycle of emotions beginning with a "comfort zone" where they feel confident, in control, and competent. They then are likely to move into what he calls the "no zone" and feel anger, resentment, frustration, and some may even attempt sabotage. They then move into the "chasm" where they may feel great anxiety, try to bargain, or even feel depressed. Finally, they move into the "go zone" where they accept the change, begin to feel excited about it, and start getting creative with the implementation. All teachers may not go through every step or feel every emotion, but it is natural for everyone to resist change, and administrators should be aware of this and prepare to support their teachers. They must be aware that change is a developmental process that takes time, even years. During the process, they will find that their teachers will be frustrated, fearful, and lost. Some may even question why they tried something new. At times, teachers need to vent, and administrators should be there to give support. The administrators should be able to determine whether to step in and assist or just let the teacher vent. In addition, they should be ready to field questions or concerns from families. Administrators should encourage parents to talk with the classroom teacher in order to gain a deeper understanding of Shared Journal and how it benefits their children.

Administrators could use professional development funds to educate teachers and staff about Shared Journal. Teachers' professional development can be designated for learning more about the process and for organizing groups to help with implementation. Being willing to work with teachers and serve on school committees will demonstrate support and give leadership to teachers as they evaluate instructional practices like Shared Journal to make sure they are aligned with the school's mission, goals, and assessment program. This hands-on involvement is what is needed when implementing a new instructional process.

When administrators show interest in and seek to learn about new practices, they demonstrate to teachers that they are open to change. Providing a supportive environment shows teachers that they have confidence in their abilities as professionals. Like administrators, teachers want their students to meet academic standards and constantly seek ways to engage students in learning. Shared Journal meets academic standards, and students will thrive in this process when it is implemented in a classroom and school where it is supported and valued.

Summary

Teachers can be strong advocates for Shared Journal. As they showcase their children's journal entries, they create an interest in others to learn more about the process. Providing opportunities to educate others and taking the time to answer questions will increase the understanding of how Shared Journal can meet the academic needs of children. Classroom visits and interactions with children are powerful ways to engage others in the process and demonstrate the benefits of Shared Journal.

References

Abbeduto, L., Warren, S. F., & Conners, F. S. (2007). Language development in Down Syndrome: From the prelinguistic period to the acquisition of literacy. *Mental Retardation and Developmental Disabilities Research Reviews, 13*, 247–261.

Adams, M. J. (1990). *Beginning to read: Thinking and learning about print* (p. 416). Urbana, IL: Center for the Study of Reading, The Reading Research and Education Center, University of Illinois at Urbana-Champaign.

Adams, M. J., Foorman, B. R, Lundberg, I., & Beeler, T. (1998a). The elusive phoneme. *American Educator, 22*(1 & 2), 18–29.

Adams, M. J., Foorman, B. R., Lundberg, I., & Beeler, T. (1998b). *Phonemic awareness in young children: A classroom curriculum.* Baltimore, MD: Paul H. Brookes.

Anderson, R. C., & Freebody, P. (1981). Vocabulary knowledge. In J. Guthrie (Ed.), *Comprehension and teaching research reviews* (pp. 77–117). Newark, DE: International Reading Association.

Anning, A., & Edwards, A. (1999). *Promoting children's learning from birth to five: Developing the new early years professional.* Buckingham: Open University Press.

Armbruster, B. B., Lehr, F., & Osborn, J. (2001). *Put reading first: The research building blocks for teaching children to read.* Washington, DC: National Institute for Literacy.

Baker, L., Dreher, M., & Guthrie, J. (2000). *Engaging young readers.* New York: The Guilford Press.

Bal, M. (Ed). (2004). *Narrative theory: Critical concepts in literary and cultural studies, Vol. 1: Major issues in narrative theory.* London: Routledge.

Barthes, R. (2004). Introduction to the structural analysis of narratives. In M. Bal (Ed.), *Narrative theory: Critical concepts in literary and cultural studies* (pp. 65–116). London: Routledge.

Bauer, E. B., & Manyak, P. C. (2008). Creating language-rich instruction for English-language learners. *The Reading Teacher, 62*(2), 176–178.

Baumann, J. F., Hoffman, J. V., Duffy-Hester, A. M., & Ro, J. M. (2000). "The First R" yesterday and today: US elementary reading instruction practices reported by teachers and administrators. *Reading Research Quarterly, 35*(3), 338–377.

Biemiller, A. (2005). Size and sequence in vocabulary development: Implications for choosing words for primary grade vocabulary instruction. In E. H. Hiebert & M. Kamil (Eds.), *Teaching and learning vocabulary: Bringing research to practice* (pp. 223–245). Mahway, NJ: Lawrence Erlbaum.

Bishop, D. V. M., & Edmundson, A. (1987). Language-impaired 4-year-olds: Distinguishing transient from persistent impairment. *Journal of Speech and Language Disorders, 2*, 156–173. (May 1987). American Speech-Language-Hearing Association.

Branscombe, N. A. (1991). *Young children's use of social and narrative thought in the construction of literary awareness.* Unpublished Doctoral Dissertation, Auburn University, AL.

Branscombe, N. A., & Taylor, J. B. (1988). "I wanna write jes like in dat book!": Talk and its role in the shared journal experience. In M. Lightfoot & N. Martin (Eds.), *The word for teaching is learning: Essays for James Britton* (pp. 107–136). Portsmouth, NH: Heinemann Educational Books.

Branscombe, N. A., & Taylor, J. (1996). The development of Scrap's understanding of written language. *Childhood Education, 72*(5), 278–281.

Branscombe, N. A., & Taylor, J. B. (2000). "It would be as good as Snow White.": Play and prosody. In K. A. Roskos & J. F. Christie (Eds.), *Play and literacy in early childhood: Research from multiple perspectives.* Mahwah, NJ: Lawrence Erlbaum.

Brimijoin, K. (2005). Differentiation and high stakes testing: An oxymoron? *Theory into Practice, 44*(3), 254–261.

Britsch, S. (1992). *The development of "Story" within the preschool.* Ann Arbor, MI: UMI.

Britton, J. (1982). *Prospect and retrospect: Selected essays of James Britton*, G. Pradl (Ed.). London: Heinemann.

Brown, R. (1973). *A first language: The early stages*. Cambridge, MA: Harvard University Press.

Bruner, J. (1984). Language, mind and reading. In H. Goelman, A. Oberg, & F. Smith (Eds.), *Awakening to literacy* (pp. 193–200). Portsmouth, NH: Heinemann.

Burkato, D., & Daehler, M. (1995). *Child development: A thematic approach*. Boston: Houghton Mifflin Company.

Cazden, C. (2001). *Classroom discourse: The language of teaching and learning* (2nd ed.). Portsmouth, NH: Heinemann.

Charman, T., Drew, A., Baird, C., & Baird, G. (2003). Measuring early language development in preschool children with autism spectrum disorder using the MacArthur Communicative Development Inventory (Infant Form). *Journal of Child Language, 30*, 213–236.

Chomsky, N. (1975). *Reflections on language*. New York: Pantheon Books.

Clay, M. M. (1991). *Becoming literate: The construction of inner control*. Auckland, New Zealand: Heinemann.

Clay, M. M. (1997). *An observation survey of early literacy achievement*. Portsmouth, NH: Heinemann.

Clay, M. M. (1998). *By different paths to common outcomes*. York, ME: Stenhouse.

Cleveland, L. (1989). *Influences on children's selection of writing topics*. Unpublished manuscript, Auburn University, AL.

Cook, G. (2000). *Language play, language learning*. Oxford, UK: Oxford University Press.

Cooper, H. (1995). *History in the early years* (2nd ed.). New York: Routledge.

Craine, K. (2007). Managing the cycle of change. *The Information Management Journal*, September/October, 44–50.

Cuthell, J. P. (2005). The impact of interactive whiteboards on teaching and learning attainment. *Proceedings of SITE 2005* (pp. 1353–1355). AACE: Phoenix, AZ.

DeVries, R., & Zan, B. (1996). Assessing interpersonal understanding in the classroom context. *Childhood Education, 72*(5), 265–268.

Doise, W., & Mugny, G. (1984). *The social development of the intellect*. New York: Pergamon Press.

Dworin, J. (2002). Examining children's biliteracy in the classroom. In A. I. Willis, G. E. Garcia, R. Barrera, & V. J. Harris (Eds.), *Multicultural issues in literacy research and practice*. New York: Lawrence Erlbaum.

Dyson, A. (1993). *Social worlds of children learning to write in an urban school*. New York: Teachers College Press.

Egan, K. (1982). Teaching history to young children. *Phi Delta Kappan, 63*, 439–441.

Elbow, P. (1998). *Writing without teachers*. New York: Oxford University Press.

Ernst, G., & Richard, K. (1995). Reading and writing pathways to conversation in the ESL classroom. *The Reading Teacher, 48*(4), 320–326.

Ferreiro, E., & Teberosky, A. (1982). *Literacy before schooling*. Portsmouth, NH: Heinemann.

Fitzgerald, J., & Shanahan, T. (2000). Reading and writing relations and their development. *Educational Psychologist, 35*, 39–50.

Freire, P. (1989). *Pedagogy of the oppressed*. New York: Continuum.

Gallas, K. (1994). *The language of learning: How children talk, write, draw, and sing their understanding of the world* (Language and Literacy Series). New York: Teachers College Press.

Gardner, H. (1980). *Artful scribbles: The significance of children's drawings*. New York: Basic Books.

Garner, T. B. (2008). *"Is it sharing day? Cuz man I got a story to tell?": Shared journal in a reading intervention program*. Unpublished manuscript, Columbus State University, Columbus, GA.

Genesee, F., Nicoladis, E., & Paradis, J. (1995). Language differentiation in early bilingual development. *Journal of Child Language, 22*, 611–631.

Genesee, F., Paradis, J., & Crago, M. B. (2004). *Dual language development and disorders: A handbook on bilingualism and second language learning*. Baltimore, MD: Brookes.

Genishi, C. (1988). Children's language: Learning words from experience. *Young Children, 44*, 16–23.

Goodman, K., & Goodman, Y. (1983). Reading and writing relationships: Pragmatic functions. *Language Arts, 60*, 590–599.

Gordon, C. (1989). Socializing the writing process through collaboration. *The Canadian Journal of English Language Arts, 12*, 3–15.

Goswami, U. (2005). Phonological and lexical processes. In M. L. Kamil, P. B. Mosenthal, P. D. Pearson, & R. Barr (Eds.), *Handbook of reading research, Vol. III* (pp. 251–267). Mahwah, NJ: Lawrence Erlbaum.

Gruber, H., & Voneche, J. (Eds.). (1995). *The essential Piaget*. Northvale, NJ: Jason Aronson Inc.

Gunnels, J. A. (1992). "Man, you know you be reading good! You know all 'dem words!": Young children's literacy acquisition during a small group intervention program. *Dissertation Abstracts International* (AAT 9310983).

Hagemann, J. (2001). A bridge from home to school: Helping working class students acquire school literacy. *The English Journal, 90*(4), 74–81.

Hall, G., & Loucks, S. (1979). *Implementing innovations in schools: A concerns-based approach.* Austin, TX: Research and Development Center for Teacher Education, University of Texas.

Hall, L. A., & Piazza, S. V. (2008). Critically reading texts: What students do and how teachers can help. *The Reading Teacher, 62*(1), 32–41.

Halliday, M. (1978) *Language as a social semiotic: The social interpretation of language and meaning.* Baltimore, MD: University Park Press.

Hart, B., & Risley, T. (1999). *The social world of children learning to talk.* Baltimore, MD: Paul H. Brooks.

Harvey, S., & Goudvis, A. (2000). *Strategies that work: Teaching comprehension to enhance understanding.* Portland, ME: Stenhouse.

Hayakaw, S. I. (1941). *Language in action* (p. 189). New York: Harcourt, Brace and Company.

Heath, S. B. (2006). *Ways with words: Language, life, and work in communities and classrooms.* Cambridge, England: Cambridge University Press.

Hiebert, E. H., Pearson, P. D., Taylor, B. M., Richardson, V., & Paris, S. G. (1998). *Every child a reader.* Ann Arbor, MI: The Center for the Improvement of Early Reading Achievement.

Hord, S., Rutherford, W., Huling-Austin, L., & Hall, G. (1987). *Taking charge of change.* Alexandria, VA: Association of Supervision and Curriculum Development.

Ives, W., & Houseworth, M. (1980). The role of standard orientations in children's drawings of interpersonal relationships: Aspects of graphic feature marking. *Society of Research in Child Development, 51,* 591–593.

Jordan, A., & Stanovich, P. (2004). The beliefs and practices of Canadian teachers about including students with special needs in their regular elementary classrooms. *Exceptionality Education Canada, 14*(2–3), 25–46.

Junker, D. A., & Stockman, I. J. (2002). Expressive vocabulary of German–English bilingual toddlers. *American Journal of Speech-Language Pathology, 11,* 381–394.

Kamii, C. (1985). *Young children reinvent arithmetic: Implications of Piaget's theory.* New York: Teachers College Press.

Kamii, C. (1989). *Young children continue to reinvent arithmetic—Second grade.* New York: Teachers College Press.

Kamii, C. (1990). *Achievement testing in the early grades: The games grownups play.* Washington, DC: National Association for the Education of Young Children.

Kamii, C. (2000). *Young children reinvent arithmetic: Implications of Piaget's theory* (2nd ed.). New York: Teacher's College Press.

Kamii, C., & Manning, M. (2002). Phonemic awareness and beginning reading and writing. *Journal of Research in Childhood Education, 17*(1), 38–46.

Kami, C., & Randazzo, M. (1985). Social interaction and invented spelling. *Language Arts, 62,* 124–132.

Knipping, N. (1991). Developing civic discourse: A second grade example. *Childhood Education, 68*(1), 14–17.

Kristoffersen, K. E. (2008). Speech and language development in cri du chat syndrome: A critical review. *Clinical Linguistics & Phonetics, 22*(6), 443–457.

Kuntay, A., & Ervin-Tripp, S. M. (1997). Conversational narratives of children: Occasions and structures. *Journal of Narrative and Life History, 7,* 113–120.

Land, L. (1998). *The role of talk in kindergarten children's construction of story.* Unpublished doctoral dissertation, Auburn University, AL.

Langer, J. (1992). Reading, writing, and genre development. In J. Truman & M. A. Doyle (Eds.), *Reading/writing connections: Learning from research* (pp. 32–54). Newark, DE: International Reading Association.

Lanter, E., & Watson, L. R. (2008). Promoting literacy in students with ASD: The basics for SLP. *Language, Speech, and Hearing Services in Schools, 39,* 33–43.

Leopold, W. F. (1939–1949). *Speech development of a bilingual child.* Evanston, IL: Northwestern University Press, 4 Vols.

Liberman, I. Y., Shankweiler, D., & Liberman, A. M. (1989). The alphabetic principle and learning to read. In D. Shankweiler & I. Y. Liberman (Eds.), *Phonology and reading disability: Solving the reading puzzle* (pp. 1–22). Ann Arbor, MI: University of Michigan Press.

Lindfors, J. (1991). *Children's language and learning* (2nd ed.). Needham Heights, MA: Allyn & Bacon.

Loveland, K., McEvoy, R., Tunali, B., & Kelley, M. (1990). Narrative storytelling in autism and Down syndrome. *British Journal of Developmental Psychology, 8,* 9–23.

Lundberg, I., Frost, J., & Peterson, O. (1988). Effects of an extensive program for stimulating phonological awareness in pre-school children. *Reading Research Quarterly, 23,* 263–284.

MacWhinney, B. (1999). *The emergence of language.* Hillsdale, NJ: Lawrence Erlbaum.

Malchiodi, C. (1998). *Understanding children's drawings.* New York: Guilford.

Mather, M., & Pollard, K. (2009). U.S. Hispanic and Asian population growth levels off. Population Reference Bureau. May 2009. http://www.prb.org/Articles/2009/hispanicasian.aspx

McCabe, A., & Bliss, L. S. (2003). *Patterns of narrative discourse.* Boston: Allyn & Bacon.

McCabe, A., & Rollins, P. R. (1994). Assessment of preschool narrative skills. *American Journal of Speech-Language Pathology, 3*(1), 45–56.

McCarthey, S., & Raphael, T. (1992). Alternative research perspectives. In J. Irwin & M. A. Doyle (Eds.), *Reading/writing connections: Learning from research* (pp. 2–30). Newark, DE: International Reading Association.

McTighe, J., & Brown, J. L. (2005). Differentiated instruction and educational standards: Is détente possible? *Theory into Practice, 44*(3), 234–244.

Miller, D., Glover, D., & Averis, D. (2003, March). *Exposure – The introduction of interactive whiteboard technology to secondary school mathematics teachers in training.* Paper presented at CERME3: Third Conference of the European Society for Research in Mathematics Education, Bellaria, Italy.

Miranda, A. E., McCabe, A., & Bliss, L. S. (1998). Jumping around and leaving things out: Dependency analysis applied to the narratives of children with specific language impairment. *Applied Psycholinguistics, 19,* 657–668.

National Council for the Social Studies. (1994). *Expectations of excellence: Curriculum standards for social studies.* Silver Spring, MD: National Council for the Social Studies.

National Council on Economic Education. (2002). *Economics America.* Bloomington, IN.

Nicolopoulou, A. (1997). Children and narratives: Toward an interpretive and sociocultural approach. In M. Bamberg (Ed.), *Narrative development: Six approaches* (pp. 179–215). Mahwah, NJ: Lawrence Erlbaum.

Nicolopoulou, A., McDowell, J., & Brockmeyer, C. (2006). Narrative play and emergent literacy: Storytelling and story-acting meet journal writing. In D. G. Singer, R. M. Golinkoff, & K. Hirsh-Pasek (Eds.), *Play equals learning.* New York: Oxford University Press.

No Child Left Behind Act of 2001, Pub. L. No. 107–110. (2002).

Norrick, N. (2004). Humor, tellability, and conarration in conversational storytelling. *Text, 24*(1), 79–111.

Oller, D. K., Eilers, R. E., Urbano, R., & Cobo-Lewis, A. B. (1997). Development of precursors to speech in infants exposed to two languages. *Journal of Child Language, 24,* 407–425.

Olson, C. K., Kutner, L., & Beresin, E. V. (2007). Children and video games: How much do we know? *Psychiatric Times, 24*(12), 41–45.

Painter, D. D., Whiting, E., & Wolters, B. (2005). The use of an interactive whiteboard in promoting interactive teaching and learning. *VSTE Journal, 19*(2), 31–40.

Pellegrini, A. D., & Galda, L. (1988). The effects of age and context on children's use of narrative language. *Research in the Teaching of English, 22*(2), 183–195.

Pellegrini, A. D., Galda, L., Bartini, M., & Charak, D. (1988). Oral language and literacy learning in context: The role of social relationships. *Merrill-Palmer Quarterly* (Jan. 1998). Found at http://findarticles.com/p/articles/mi_qa3749/is_199801/ai_n8779566/pg_2/?tag=content;col1

Peregoy, S. F., & Boyle, O. F. (2005). *Reading, writing, and learning in ESL.* Boston: Allyn & Bacon.

Perret-Clermont, A. (1980). *Social interaction and cognitive development in children.* London: Academic Press.

Perry, B., & Pollard, D. (1997). Altered brain development following global neglect in early childhood. *Society for Neuroscience: Proceedings from Annual Meeting,* New Orleans, LA.

Petitto, L., Katerelos, M., Levy, B., Guana, K., Tetreault, K., & Ferraro, V. (2001). Bilingual signed and spoken language acquisition from birth: Implications for the mechanisms underlying early bilingual language acquisition. *Journal of Child Language, 28,* 453–496.

Phillips, L. (1999). *The role of storytelling in early literacy development.* ERIC ED 444147.

Piaget, J. (1932). *The moral judgment of the child.* London: Routledge & Kegan Paul.

Piaget, J. (1952). *The child's conception of number.* London: Routledge & Kegan Paul.

Piaget, J. (1962). *Play, dreams, and imitation in childhood.* New York: Norton.

Piaget, J. (1969). Science of education and the psychology of the child. New York: Viking Press.

Piaget, J. (1970). *Genetic epistemology.* New York: Columbia University Press.

Piaget, J. (1976). The affective unconscious and the cognitive unconscious. In B. Inhelder & H. H. Chapman (Eds.), *Piaget and his school: A reader in developmental psychology* (pp. 63–71). New York: Springer-Verlag.

Piaget, J. (1977). *The essential Piaget* (H. Gruber & J. Voneche, Eds.). New York: Basic Books.

Piaget, J. (1983). Piaget's theory. In P. Mussen (Ed.). *Handbook of Child Psychology* (4th edn, Vol. 1). New York: Wiley.

Piaget, J., & Inhelder, B. (1969). *The psychology of the child.* New York, Basic Books.

Pinker, S. (1994). *The language instinct: How the mind creates language.* New York: HarperCollins.

Pruden, S., Golinkoff, R., & Hennon, E. (2006). The birth of words: Ten-month-olds learn words through perceptual salience. *Child Development, 77,* 266–280.

Robertson, K., & Ford, K. (2008). *Language acquisition: An overview.* http://www.colorincolorado.org/article/26751

Ronjat, J. (1913). *Le developement du language observe chez un enfant bilingue.* Paris: Champion.

Rushton, S. (2001). Applying brain research to create developmentally appropriate learning environments. *Young Children, 56*(5), 76–82.

Sarason, S. B. (1974). *The psychological sense of community: Prospects for a community psychology.* San Francisco, CA: Jossey Bass.

Selman, R. (1980). *The growth of interpersonal understanding.* New York: Academic Press.

Sendak, M. (1998). *Where the wild things are.* New York: HarperCollins.

Silvern, S., Taylor, J. B., Williamson, P., Surbeck, E., & Kelley, M. (1986). Young children's story recall as a product of play, story familiarity, and adult intervention. *Merrill-Palmer Quarterly, 32,* 73–85.

Sinclair, H. (1991, March). Symbolic play: Its importance for the teacher and the child. Keynote address given for the College of Education at the University of Alabama Birmingham.

Snow, C. E., Porche, M. V., Tabors, P. O., & Harris, S. R. (2007). *Is literacy enough?* Baltimore, MD: Brookes.

Stadler, M. A., & Ward, G. C. (2005). Supporting the narrative development of young children. *Early Childhood Education Journal, 33*(2), 73–80.

Stambak, M., & Sinclair, H. (1993). *Pretend play among 3-year-olds.* Mahway, NJ: Lawrence Erlbaum.

Stanovich, K. E. (1993). Romance and reality. *The Reading Teacher, 47,* 280–291.

Steigler, J. W., & Hiebert, J. (1999). *The teaching gap: Best ideas from the world's teachers for improving education in the classroom.* New York: Free Press.

Stevens, E., Blake, J., Vitale, G., & McDonald, S. (1998). Mother–infant object involvement at 9 and 15 months: Relation to infant cognition and vocabulary. *First Language, 18,* 203–222.

Swan, K., Schenker, J., & Kratcoski, A., (2007). The effects of the use of interactive whiteboards on student achievement. Retrieved from http://www.iprase.tn.it/attivit%E0/studio_e_ricerca/red5_08/download/07_The_Effects_of_the_Use_of_Interactive_Whiteboards_on_Student_Achievement.pdf

Tabors, P. O. (1997). *One child, two languages: A guide for preschool educators of children learning English as a second language.* Baltimore, MD: Brookes.

Taylor, J., & Cleveland, L. (1986). *A qualitative look at shared journal writing in a kindergarten classroom.* Paper presented at the meeting of the American Educational Research Association, San Francisco, CA.

Tomlinson, C. A. (2004). Differentiation in diverse settings: A consultant's experiences in two similar school districts. *School Administrator, 61*(7), 28–36.

Torgesen, J. K. (1998). Catch them before they fall. *American Educator, 22*(1 & 2), 32–39.

Vacca, R. T., & Vacca, J. L. (2002). Study guides. *Content Area Reading, 2,* 342–348.

van't Hooft, M., Swan, K., Cook, D., & Lin, Y. (2007). What is ubiquitous computing? In M. van't Hooft & K. Swan (Eds.), *Ubiquitous computing in education: Invisible technology, visible impact* (pp. 3–18). New York: Routledge.

Vernon, S. (1993). Initial sound/letter correspondences in children's early written productions. *Journal of Research in Childhood Education, 8*(1), 12–22.

Vernon, S., & Ferreiro, E. (1999). Writing development: A neglected variable in the consideration of phonological awareness. *Harvard Educational Review, 69*(4), 395–415.

Volterra, V., & Taeschner, T. (1978). The acquisition and development of language by bilingual children. *Journal of Child Language, 5,* 311–326.

Vygotsky, L. S. (1976). Play and its role in the mental development of the child. In J. Brunner, A. Jolly, & K. Sylva (Eds.), *Play: Its role in development and evolution* (pp. 537–554). New York: Basic Books.

Vygotsky, L. S. (1978). *Mind in society: The development of higher psychological processes.* Cambridge, MA: Harvard University Press.

Wadsworth, B. (1971). *Piaget's theory of cognitive development.* New York: McKay.

Wagner, R. K., Torgesen, J. K., Rashotte, C. A., Hecht, S. A., Barker, T. A., Burgess, S. R., Donahue, J., & Garon, T. (1997). Changing causal relations between phonological processing abilities and word-level reading as children develop from beginning to fluent readers: A five-year longitudinal study. *Developmental Psychology, 33,* 468–479.

Walsh, C. (Ed.). (1991). *Literacy as praxis: Culture, language and pedagogy.* Norwood, NJ: Ablex.

Ward, S. (2001) *Baby talk.* New York: Ballantine Books.

Wells, G. (1986). *The meaning makers: Children learning language and using language to learn.* Portsmouth, NH: Heinemann.

Wesson, K. A. (2003). Early brain development and learning. Retrieved from http://www.sciencemaster.com/columns/wesson/wesson_early_01.php

Wolf, M. (2009). New research on an old problem: A brief history of fluency. New York: Scholastic. Retrieved from http://www2.scholastic.com/browse/article.jsp?id=4468

Zimmerman, F. J., Gilkerson, J., Richards, J., Christakis, D. A., Xu, D., Gray, S., & Yapanel, U. (2009). Teaching by listening: The importance of adult–child conversations to language development. *Pediatrics, 124,* 342–349.

Zimmerman, S., & Hutchins, C. (2003). *Seven keys to comprehension.* New York: Three Rivers Press.

Contributor Biographies

Sandy Armstrong has experience teaching in public schools as a kindergarten teacher and as an Instructional Technology Coach. Dr. Janet Taylor, the developer of Shared Journal, was her major professor for her B.S. and Master's degrees. Sandy has implemented Shared Journal in her classrooms (including bilingual classes she taught in Houston, Texas). Her expertise is in the integration of technology in early childhood classrooms. She is a SMART Exemplary Educator and a SMART Certified Master Trainer and is also an Intel Teach to the Future Master Teacher Trainer. She has created and sold a SMART Board interactive whiteboard curriculum for pre-K to second grade, Title I, and Special Education and has also used technology to work with classrooms around the world, including a literacy mentoring program. One of the schools where Sandy worked, Auburn Early Education Center, has been recognized for excellence in early childhood education, as evidenced by numerous awards.

Nancy Amanda Branscombe is an Assistant Professor of Early Childhood Education at Athens State University in Athens, Alabama. She earned a B.S. in English Education, an M.Ed. in Educational Leadership, and an Ed.D. in Early Childhood Education from Auburn University, Auburn, Alabama. She also received an M.S. in Community Counseling from Georgia State University in Atlanta, Georgia, and an M.A. from Bread Loaf School of English at Middlebury College in Middlebury, Vermont. She has offered professional presentations about Shared Journal nationally and internationally. She has published textbooks and articles on constructivist education and teacher and student action research. In addition to her collegiate teaching, Branscombe has directed Child Development Centers and Summer Enrichment programs.

Jan Gunnels Burcham is Professor of Early Childhood Education and holds the Fletcher Distinguished Chair in Teacher Education at Columbus State University. She received a B.S. and Ph.D. in Early Childhood Education from Auburn University and an M.A. in Early Childhood Education from the University of Alabama at Birmingham. She has completed numerous professional presentations nationally, as well as internationally in China and England. In addition to her faculty responsibilities, she has served as Early Childhood Program Coordinator and Director of a Summer Enrichment Program for young children.

Angela Carr is a National Board Certified teacher with a B.S. and a Master's in Early Childhood Education. She has experience teaching in public schools in Kindergarten, second grade, and Multi-Age (K, first and second) classes. Dr. Janet Taylor was her mentor for her B.S. as well as her Master's degree. Angela has implemented Shared Journal in her classroom more for than 15 years and has given presentation on Shared Journal at numerous state and national conferences. She maintains that Shared Journal has enabled her to meet the needs of her students while meeting the requirements of the State Department and her school system. Angela's area of expertise is in communicating to administrators the benefits of constructivist teaching by documenting and illustrating how it fulfills the requirements of the State Course of Study. She partners with Dr. Amanda Branscombe to provide a model constructivist classroom for Athens State University students.

Lilli Land is a National Distinguished Principal for the state of Alabama and an education consultant. She received a B.S., M.Ed., Ed.S., and Ph.D. in Early Childhood Education from Auburn University. She was formerly a kindergarten and second grade teacher and coordinator for kindergarten, student assessment, and federal programs for Tallapoosa County Schools in Alabama. She was Principal of Auburn Early Education Center (AEEC), Auburn City Schools, in Auburn, Alabama. She was one of two principals in the state to receive the 2004 Alfa Principal Award, and she received the 2006 Distinguished Library Service Award for School Administrators in Alabama. Under her leadership, AEEC was named an Intel School of Distinction for Literary Achievement, a Blue Ribbon Lighthouse School, a SMART Technologies Showcase School, a Council for Leaders in Alabama Schools Banner School, and the International Reading Association Exemplary Reading Program Award winner for Alabama. AEEC was featured in a George Lucas documentary, "Beginning the Journey: Five-Year-Olds Drive Their Own PBL Projects."

Allyson Martin has teaching experience as a kindergarten teacher and as a reading coach. Allyson was a student of Dr. Janet Taylor, the author of the Shared Journal curriculum. As a reading coach, she is fortunate to work in a school that implements Shared Journal school-wide, and she frequently spends time in classrooms observing interactions and storytelling during the sharing process, conferencing with children about their pictorial and written story representations, and working with teachers to assess students' literacy acquisition through Shared Journal. Allyson's school, Auburn Early Education Center, has been recognized for excellence in early childhood education, as evidenced by numerous awards. She has modeled Shared Journal for novice teachers and coached them in the implementation of this process in their classrooms and has presented Shared Journal for other schools within the Auburn City School System, schools systems in other parts of the state, visitors from other states, and at various conferences.

Janet B. Taylor is Wayne T. Smith Distinguished Professor Emeritus of Early Childhood Education. She was formerly a kindergarten, first, second, and third grade teacher for 15 years. She earned her Ph.D. in Early Childhood Education at the Florida State University. At Auburn University she taught at the undergraduate, master's and doctoral level and served as the coordinator of the Early Childhood graduate and undergraduate programs in Curriculum and Teaching for many years. Her teaching and research specializations are in curriculum design, young children's learning, and constructivist explanations of learning. She originated the Shared Journal, now being implemented in early childhood settings throughout the world, and served as guest editor of the Association of Childhood Education International's *Childhood Education*, 1996 theme issue *Understanding Children's Understanding*. She has co-authored two texts: *Early Childhood Education: A Constructivist Perspective* and *Early Childhood Curriculum: A Constructivist Perspective*, the latter of which has been reviewed as one of the leading curriculum texts in early childhood education and has been translated for use in Korea. In addition to these two texts, she has co-authored and/or authored over 26 publications. One of those publications, *The Global Bridges Curriculum* is currently being used in Chinese schools. In 1998, she was awarded the Outstanding Early Childhood Teacher Educator Award by the National Association of Early Childhood Teacher Educators and, in 2001, she was named a Wayne T. Smith Distinguished Professor at Auburn University.

Index

Note: page numbers in **bold** refer to illustrations

Down's syndrome children 120
drawing: representational 8–9, **9**, 11; in Shared
  Journals 25–6, 34–5, 85–6, 87, 92, 123

early language learning 4–7; adult role in 11–13;
  difficulties 16
earth sciences: understanding 78
economics: understanding 74
editing: by teachers 132–4
emotions: and change 146–7; handling 143
end at high point narrative **137**
English language learners (ELLs) 15; helped by
  use of interactive whiteboards 113, 114; and
  Shared Journal 123
Ernst, G. 123

fairness 75
family–teacher conferences 132
figurative language 63
fluency 48–9
formal operational stage **4**

Garner, T. B. 123–6
geography: understanding 73–4, 137
government: understanding 71–3
grading 135–6, **138**
Gunnels, J. A. 123, 126–7

"happy" hypothesis 23
hearing difficulties: and Shared Journal 122
historians: methods 71, 138–9
history: assessment 138–9; understanding
  69–71
hypotheses: and spoken language recording
  86–7; and story conceptions 23–4

if–then constructions 59
imitation: deferred 8
improvisation 61
"Information Organizer" 113, 114, 120
interactive whiteboards 112–16; advantages
  112; calendar 112–13; English language
  learners (ELLs) helped by use of 113, 114; for
  key words of stories 114; microphone tool
  use 114; for negotiation 115; and questioning
  114; recording 113, 114, 115; for sharing
  with class 113–14; for signing up to share
  112–13; special needs children use of 115; for
  titles of stories 114; for voting 115; writing
  on 114
intervention classes 123–7; attitudes
  improvement 125–6; collaboration 127;
  modifications to Shared Journal process
  124–6; plan devising 132; writing
  improvement 125, 126–7

journal writing checklists 136, **138**
justice 75

Kamii, C. 22, 76
kindergarten class representations in Shared
  Journal 84–7, 90–6
knowledge of self and others 66–8

Land, L. 23, 56
language arts 33
language arts (literacy) curriculum: alignment
  with Shared Journal 102, **103–4**
language learning 3–4; adult role in 11–13;
  after sensorimotor stage 9–11; bilingual 14;
  development in 4–7; difficulties 16; through
  play 13, *see also* early language learning
language qualities 42–3
leap-frog narrative **137**
letter-name hypothesis 87, 91, 92
letters to parents 29, **30**, 31, **31**, 144
life sciences: understanding 77–8
Lindford, J. 35, 37
listening 37–8
literacy development: and Shared Journal
  experiences 45
Literacy Intervention Program 124
literacy (language arts) curriculum: alignment
  with Shared Journal 102, **103–4**
literary constructions 58–65; if–then
  constructions 59; language of literature and
  prose use 61–5; perspective taking through
  improvisation 61; reflection 59–60
literary qualities 42

McCabe, A. 135
McTighe, J. 83
Manyak, P. C. 123
mathematics 75–7, 136, 137
mean length utterance 7
mental images 9
Miranda, A. E. 135
miscellaneous narrative **137**
modeling: by teachers 134–5
moral compass 75
moral dilemmas 75
moral realism 75
moral relativism 75
motherese 5, 12

narrative development: assessment 135, **137**;
  checklists 135, **137**
narrative rubrics 135, **136**, 137
narrative voice: development through social
  interactions 58–65; oral 52; written 53–4
narrative voice construction 51; stages 54–8